ALL WORST THE HUMANS

ALL THE WORST WORST HUMANS

How I Made News for Dictators, Tycoons, and Politicians

PHIL ELWOOD

Henry Holt and Company
New York

Henry Holt and Company
Publishers since 1866
120 Broadway
New York, New York 10271
www.henryholt.com

Library of Congress Cataloging-in-Publication Data

Names: Elwood, Phil (Philip) author.
Title: All the worst humans : how I made news for dictators, tycoons,
    and politicians / Phil Elwood.
Description: First edition. | New York : Henry Holt and Company,
    2024. | Includes bibliographical references.
Identifiers: LCCN 2023055958 | ISBN 9781250321572 (hardcover) |
    ISBN 9781250321589 (ebook)
Subjects: LCSH: Elwood, Phil (Philip) | Public relations and
    politics. | Communication in politics. | Political consultants—
    United States—Biography. | Public relations consultants—
    United States—Biography.
Classification: LCC JA85.2.U6 E58 2024 | DDC 659.2/9320092
    [B]—dc23/eng/20231228
LC record available at https://lccn.loc.gov/2023055958

Our books may be purchased in bulk for promotional, educational, or
business use. Please contact your local bookseller or the Macmillan
Corporate and Premium Sales Department at (800) 221-7945, exten-
sion 5442, or by e-mail at MacmillanSpecialMarkets@macmillan.com.

First Edition 2024

Designed by Omar Chapa

Printed in the United States of America

1   3   5   7   9   10   8   6   4   2

For Lindsay, who really took the
"for better or worse" thing seriously

The single biggest problem in communication is the illusion that it has taken place.

—GEORGE BERNARD SHAW

AUTHOR'S NOTE

This is my story, as I remember it. Some names and a few details have been changed to protect the many guilty and the few innocents.

PROLOGUE

FEBRUARY 8, 2018

When the FBI knocks, you are going to lose. It's just a question of what. And how much of it. Money. Love. Freedom. Friends. Jobs. If they knock, you have been gambling. And you do not have the high card in this hand.

At 6:30 a.m., my phone rings. I mute CNN's Chris Cuomo discussing the latest in Robert Mueller's election interference inquiry and answer to make the ringing stop.

"Phil Elwood?" a woman's voice says. "This is Special Agent Logan with the FBI."

"Good morning?"

"Do you still live at apartment one-zero-zero-eight?"

"Not anymore," I say, struggling to process. "We've moved within the building."

"What apartment are you in right now?"

I look at my wife, Lindsay. She is still in her pajamas,

answering emails from a higher education reporter. Fighting the good fight. "Can you give me an hour?" I ask Agent Logan.

Fight-or-flight kicks in. Protect what matters. "Lindsay, the FBI is downstairs," I say. "They will be up in one hour. You need to leave."

My wife speaks with the lyrical precision, and efficiency, of a machine gun. When her adrenaline spikes, the words get really fast. So, I can't repeat with any accuracy the chain of concern, profanity, and fear that comes out of her. She is out the door in record time.

I have thirty minutes before the agents are due to knock. Normally, the FBI doesn't call ahead, so I believe I am unique in my ability to describe how one waits for them. How would you spend your time? I read their Wikipedia entry. Thirty-five thousand employees, $9.8 billion annual budget, thirteen thousand Special Agents, many of whom carry the Glock 19 Gen5, a 9mm with a fifteen-round magazine. A top priority of today's Federal Bureau of Investigation: "Protect the United States against foreign intelligence operations, espionage, and cyber operations."

At this moment, there is a bag in my closet full of promotional material for an Israel-based organization that advertises that it is a "foreign intelligence operation" that engages in "online operations." The word *espionage* is not in the brochure, but it is strongly implied.

Ten minutes to go. I think about the million dollars the Israelis have moved through my bank account. The wire transfers to the Seychelles, Cyprus, Switzerland, the

Caribbean, Palestine, and who knows where else. About the laptop whirring away under the desk in my office, which the Israelis told me never to touch. Five minutes. I worry about the reach of the Wire Fraud Act, and of the Espionage Act of 1917. My pajama bottoms peek out from under the legs of my cargo pants.

Then comes the knock.

I open the door to a man and a woman wearing pistols on their hips. The woman steps forward and hands me her business card: "Special Agent Logan, Counterproliferation." It is my understanding that this division works to stop the proliferation of nuclear weapons. I also understand that my life is about to change. Until this morning, I've been a ghost. My name has never even appeared in a *Politico* "Spotted" blurb. Google "Phil Elwood," and you'll find a dead jazz reviewer for the *San Francisco Chronicle*.

I offer the agents coffee. They decline. I walk them to my dining room table. They sit down across from me. Their body language telegraphs: the *government versus you*.

"Mr. Elwood," Agent Logan begins. "Do you know why we're here?"

Several things come to mind. It could be the Israelis. Or Muammar Gaddafi. Or Bashar al-Assad. Or the Iranians. Or because of what I pulled in Antigua. Or the bank transfers to accounts in tax havens all over the world. Or Project Rome. Probably not the ounce of cannabis in my kitchen drawer.

They could be knocking on my door about so many things I've done over the last two decades in public relations.

ALL WORST
THE HUMANS

CHAPTER 1

Of Marble and Giants

EIGHTEEN YEARS EARLIER, JULY 2000

The halls of the Capitol Building are empty this morning. The clinks of the liquor bottles in the hand truck I'm pushing are the only sound. I love being alone here, marveling at marble columns propping up carved ceilings. Under the massive dome of the Rotunda, paintings tell the mythology of early America. In Statuary Hall, I nod to a bronze statue of Huey Long, an assassinated senator who some consider a hero, others a criminal, and then enter a wood-paneled corridor. Spiral staircases of iron and marble materialize out of dark corners.

I maneuver the bottles past unmarked doors that lead to the hideaway offices of Senators Trent Lott, Mitch McConnell, and Ted Kennedy. Senators steal away to these coveted havens to host meetings they'd rather not have eyeballed by reporters or to nap after marathon debates. The booze is heavy, and I'm out of breath when I reach Sen. Daniel Patrick Moynihan's hideaway. Vodka soda sweat leaks through my cheap, white collared shirt. We interns were out late at Politiki bar last night.

I let myself in and head for the brass bar cart. Fifths of whiskey, gin, scotch, and Tio Pepe sherry, Moynihan's favorite, get loaded in and lined up. When I'm finished, I sit on a leather couch dyed the same dark mahogany as the regal desk and spark up a Camel. Moynihan is a fellow smoker. His hideaway reeks of tobacco.

The hundred or so hideaways in the Capitol are passed down through handshake deals. Seniority rules, and sitting on the Finance Committee doesn't hurt. Junior senators fight over windowless basement rooms the size of utility closets and furnished with cots. Moynihan has earned a view of Pennsylvania Avenue and space for ten people to sip cocktails. Standing under an oil painting, I pull back the cream-colored curtains and take it all in. I imagine the senator from New York in here, lighting up, pouring a tumbler of Tio Pepe, and telling stories about the presidents he has advised.

Sitting in the private office of a Senate demigod still doesn't feel real. I'm a twenty-year-old college dropout whose only credentials are a job at a Mexican restaurant and a cocaine problem. The rest of my intern class are the kids of campaign donors and New York City's financial glitterati. My dad is a pastor in the *other* Washington. He preaches to a congregation in Olympia.

Six months ago, I was a sophomore at the University of Pittsburgh on a debate scholarship. Debate is about speed. Being able to talk fast was the prerequisite for entry. On weekends, I traveled to universities around the nation to argue about what policies would lead to nuclear war. Rapid-fire reading of news clippings scored points in a round. So did biting insults lodged at your opponent in an attempt to trap them in a rhetorical mishap. You won by manipulating the news and calling it "evidence" to advance your argument. I won a lot.

My grades were nearly perfect until I started working nights as a cook at Mad Mex. The waiters survived on a diet of wings and cocaine. One night, one of them noticed that I seemed a bit down and he offered me a pick-me-up from his bag. It worked. For fifteen minutes. Three months later, I was failing five out of five courses. I don't believe I attended one.

The week before finals, I called my older brother in a panic. He jumped on a plane to Pittsburgh. We debated my options. I tried to advance the argument for my brother taking my finals. It was raining when we went to the registrar's office and filled out the forms. The first Elwood to drop out of college.

My parents collected me at SeaTac airport. I deplaned drunk on whiskey and clutching a plush toy of Opus the Penguin, from Berkeley Breathed's comic strip. My father shook his head and made me see a shrink. I snowballed my way through the sessions. Left out the cocaine use. The shrink informed me that I was suffering from "situational depression."

"Since you are removed from the situation," she explained. "The problem must be resolved."

"Makes sense," I said.

It didn't. And the depression didn't lift. A childhood friend, who I'll call Preston, worried that I had no prospects after dropping out of school, threw me a lifeline. His college classmate Eric, a trust fund kid, worked in Washington, DC, as Senator Moynihan's aide. If he liked me, Eric could get me an internship on the Hill.

I called Eric, and he told me to meet him the next Tuesday, at 10 p.m., at 1823 M Street. "*Northwest* M Street, the one near the White House," he said. "Do you have a fake ID?"

"Indeed I do."

"Bring it. You'll need it in DC," Eric said. "Your official interview will be on the Hill the next day. But this one is more important. I vet the interns for the staff."

My parents bought me a suit at the mall, and I flew to Washington. Résumé in hand, I cabbed it to a redbrick building with blacked-out windows on M Street. My fake ID fooled the bouncer. Inside, Ice Cube's "You Can Do It" played as a dancer sprayed Windex on the pole before taking off her underwear. A topless woman asked if I wanted some singles.

Eric wasn't hard to spot. He was the only other guy wearing a suit in the strip club on a Tuesday night. He chugged a Bud Light at a table with a clear view of the stage. I handed him my résumé. He gave it to a dancer in a neon-yellow G-string.

"Relax," he said, sliding me a beer. "You met me at Camelot on a Tuesday night. You passed the test."

In Moynihan's hideaway, I kill my cigarette and flush it down the toilet. I lock up, push the empty hand truck past Minority Leader Tom Daschle's office, and ride an elevator down to the basement. I flash my badge to a guard, cut through the crypt under the Rotunda, and head into the Capitol Hill Tunnels. I love these underground passageways, that feeling of special access.

I walk the pedestrian pathway alongside a miniature subway trolley modeled after the Disney World Monorail. A group of congressional aides are taking the two-minute ride, briefcases on their laps. To my right, I spot Sen. Fred Thompson.

"Good afternoon, Senator," I say. "*Die Hard Two* was on TNT last night."

"Was it really?" he replies in the deep southern drawl that was so out of place when he played a New York district attorney on NBC's *Law & Order*. "Walk me back to my office."

On the twenty-minute trip to the Hart Building, Thompson asks whether I think DC or Hollywood is the more terrifying place. I argue in favor of Hollywood. The Capitol doesn't frighten me. Just the opposite. From the moment I set foot in DC, I knew I was home. The Hill is a real-world version of debate team. Everyone talks fast, and there are winners, losers, and nukes. Last week, I had a drink with Sen. Russ Feingold, who told me stories of working with John McCain and Carl Levin on trying to pass campaign finance reform. I've gone from bussing tables at a Mexican restaurant in Pittsburgh to rubbing elbows with senators. I never want to leave.

I weave through redbrick-walled tunnels back toward Moynihan's staff office in the Russell Building. Discarded and broken office furniture lines the bowels of the Capitol Hill office buildings. I pass the Senate barbershop, where I recently got a bad haircut sitting next to Majority Leader Lott. A quick elevator ride up from the basement takes me to Russell's fourth floor, where I drop off the hand truck and head down a flight of stairs to a private parking lot.

Two interns are already out here smoking. The senior senator from Michigan Carl Levin's beaten-up blue Oldsmobile sticks out among the rows of luxury sedans. I smoke another Camel and watch Kit Bond of Missouri climb out of a black town car. Kay Bailey Hutchison struts by, followed by her "purse boys," two young, attractive male aides who carry her luxury bags around Capitol Hill. When senators bum a smoke before hustling to their next meeting, I feel like a young Henry Hill parking cars for Paulie's crew in *Goodfellas*.

It's almost four o'clock. In this town, the most important hour is happy hour. I head back out into the muggy city, down

First Street, passing the Supreme Court and the Library of Congress, where 3,700 boxes of Moynihan's personal papers have been kept for posterity. It's the largest one-man collection in the library, Moynihan's legislative director recently told me over whiskey and Cokes at the Capitol Lounge.

At Pennsylvania Avenue, a helicopter buzzes across the sky. The pilot shadows a motorcade of black SUVs careening downtown, lights flashing and sirens blaring. When the street clears, I duck into the Hawk 'n' Dove. I nurse a vodka soda, holding a good table with a view of the TVs, tuned to CNN. Just like the hideaway office system, this place runs on dibs. Soon the bar will be teaming with staffers from both sides of the aisle. They will drink, party, date, and sometimes put together bipartisan legislation. Tables are valuable currency. As an intern, I take it as my sacred duty to make sure the staff doesn't have to stand at the bar.

At five o'clock, Moynihan's staff trickles into Hawk 'n' Dove in ascending order of the food chain. Legislative correspondents arrive first, along with the rest of the interns. An hour later, the legislative assistants claim their seats. Then come the legislative director and, finally, around seven, Moynihan's chief of staff. His blue suit is rumpled, and he looks exhausted. In his hand is today's "clip sheet," a binder compiling daily press filings that mention our boss. The interns create it each morning by cutting apart the *Washington Post*, the *New York Times*, and the hyper-local weeklies and meticulously underlining Moynihan's name.

"Thanks for holding down the fort, Phil," the chief of

staff says. "Look at this. Hillary Clinton is going to walk into Moynihan's seat. Rick Lazio doesn't stand a chance."

I've landed in Moynihan's office just in time. He's about to retire after twenty-four years in the Senate. The alumni list from his office reads like a who's who of Washington, DC—and they help each other out. I spent the rest of the summer helping *them* out by following the legislative director's instructions: "Do anything we ask. And do it with a smile. Even if it's not part of your job. Even if it's weird." I take his words to heart. Moynihan's staff takes a shine to me because I volunteer to huff cartloads of Tio Pepe and get menial intern tasks done at my restaurant pace.

There are two ways to go about a career here: get in deeper or get out. I know one thing: I'm never leaving Washington. But a college dropout's trajectory is limited; I need a degree. Before my internship ends, I apply to George Washington University. I draft my own letter of recommendation, and Moynihan's chief of staff, for whom I've held tables all summer at half the bars in town, signs it. "Motivated and gifted with his words, Phil Elwood will make a valuable addition to your storied university."

I wake up in a holding cell. Two cops yank me into an interrogation room and slam me with the accusation that I drunkenly crashed through a window at GWU's Gelman Library. I can't remember last night, but my throbbing head and the cuts on my body indicate that the police are telling the truth. I'm frog-marched into a sheriff's van and handcuffed to the floor.

I stand in front of a judge, who tells me he knows I'm very sorry for what I've done and that I will never do it again. He slaps me on the wrist with twenty hours of community service. Later, I hear that Moynihan's office made a call. A few days after I get home from central booking, a thin letter arrives from George Washington. I am no longer welcome on campus.

I'm certain I'll be excommunicated from DC. I'll have to return to Olympia. My parents will once again watch their son emerge at the Arrivals gate holding his plush toy Opus the Penguin, like a deadbeat Sisyphus. Instead, I'm promoted. Moynihan's office makes one call, and I'm hired as a legislative correspondent for the senior senator from Michigan, Carl Levin. The happy hours continue. It's amazing I get anything done with all the booze. Toward the end of my first year, the chief of staff hauls me into his office.

"I strongly suggest you get a college degree," he says. "George Washington is off the table, clearly. What about Georgetown?"

Given my high school C average, Georgetown should be off the table, too. But it turns out Levin has considerable influence with the university. One letter from the senator and I'm accepted as a transfer student. I realize this is how the world works, or at least how this world does. It is not a meritocracy.

In the basement office of the Permanent Subcommittee on Investigations, staffers drop off crates of documents. "Go through these. Look for anything suspicious," they instruct. They leave to fetch more boxes. Levin is leading an inquiry into the malfeasance of Enron's board of directors. Enron's spectacular implosion has been a lead story on CNN for months. Now Levin is making it his mission to codify the company's wrongdoing into the national record.

I drink coffee with a team of lawyers who haven't seen the light of day in weeks and sift through thousands of pages of emails with a highlighter. Most of the material is banal talk about steakhouse lunches and corporate retreats. Every few pages, I notice the obscene dollar amounts of Enron's transactions. Villains get paid in numbers with extra zeros.

On the day of the Enron hearings, I go watch the fireworks at the Hart Building. A homeless man stands at the front of a long line stretching down Constitution Avenue. I watch a sharky-looking guy in a jet-black suit hand the homeless man a ten-dollar bill and slide into his place. Lobbyists have probably been pulling this trick since the Grant administration. I flash my staff ID and follow the lobbyist past security and into the Senate hearing room, where I stand against the back wall.

Levin strides up to the dais in a baggy suit, the last of his hair combed over a sun-spotted scalp. In 2013, *BuzzFeed News* will publish a list of the "23 Most Important Combovers of Congress." Levin will come in second place. A man of the people. He's the hardest-working member of his staff. I watch, rapt, as he rakes Herbert Winokur Jr., Enron's

Finance Committee chair, over the coals about a half-billion-dollar loan.

"Now, when you met with my staff, did you also tell my staff you did not have much recollection of that transaction?" Levin asks, peering down his glasses, pushed far down the bridge of his nose.

"Yes, sir."

"Now that you have refreshed your recollections. Enron was borrowing a half a billion dollars from Citibank, but it did not show up on the balance sheet of Enron as debt but rather as preferred shares, which looked more like equity than debt. It was a loan disguised as equity in order to avoid showing debt on the books."

"Sir, I believe it was accounted for as a consolidated subsidiary with a—"

Levin cuts him off. "Was it shown as a loan?"

"It was shown as—the entity was consolidated and the $500 million of Citibank was a minority interest."

"But was it shown as a loan?"

Levin's got him dead to rights. I watch Winokur break. "No, sir."

An exchange worthy of a headline. I spot a gaggle of reporters taking notes at the side of the chamber. As in a debate, they've got their evidence. Now they'll print it in tomorrow's paper. And some college debater will use the article as evidence in a round where the topic is "fiscal regulation." It's codified into the record. The truth, as far as anyone is concerned.

I'm fascinated by this bloodbath, particularly by the criminals on the witness stand. Who helps them? Who prepped them for this massacre? Whoever it was, they aren't good enough at their job. Where's the consistent messaging? Why weren't they expecting these questions? Why aren't they repeating the same five lines over and over and over? Why are they just giving easy sound bites to the senator and the media?

I realize I'm probably the only person in the world who has this reaction to the Enron scandal.

I lean out into K Street, hailing a cab. It's the first week of summer. School is out. I've been barhopping with Hill staffers. A yellow cab pulls up, and I attempt to hop over a Jersey barrier. My foot catches the edge. I spin as I fall to the curb.

I can't walk. I crawl into the cab's backseat and tell the driver to take me to the nearest trauma center. When we arrive at George Washington University's ER, nurses put me in a wheelchair. Three hours later, a tech looks at my X-ray, says, "Oh shit," and starts to run out of the room. I grab his arm. Make him show me the image. The ball of my hip is floating, completely separated from my femur.

I wake up sucking oxygen from a tube. My mother is sitting in a chair next to the bed. My mother lives on the other side of the country, so I figure something is probably wrong. I don't remember anything after looking at the X-ray.

I'm on crutches for a month. Then I graduate to a cane. For the rest of my life, I'll walk with a slight limp. And the three titanium screws in my hip will ache when the temperature dips below forty degrees. A few months later, I skydive out of an airplane for the first time. At a checkup, I inform my surgeon that he must have done some good work. He is not pleased.

My parents fly in for Georgetown's graduation ceremony. They seem relieved that I made it to the finish line. Levin writes yet another letter, and I'm accepted into the London School of Economics. I live in a flat in Notting Hill, attending lectures on trade wars with the kids of prime ministers and international diplomats.

One day, I'm walking on campus when I pass a balding young man with hard eyes flanked by massive bodyguards. I've heard about Saif Gaddafi. The students whisper that he's a dictator's son. I've heard we share a weed dealer.

In a few years, he'll be one of my clients. Long after I've been on his family's payroll, the world will find out that Saif allegedly bought his PhD in philosophy from LSE with millions of pounds in bribes. Howard Davies, the distinguished institution's director, whose signature is on my diploma, will resign, disgraced.

But I'm getting ahead of myself.

I walk through the doors of Venture, which feels like the smallest public relations shop in DC. I've been back in town for a few weeks, applying for any job that will keep me close to the action on the Hill. I've missed this city. Missed working on projects that I'd read about in the newspapers the next day. Missed the happy hours spent trading gossip about senators and feeling like a master of the universe.

Venture's office isn't much more than a few desks scattered in the basement of a lobbying firm. A young woman shakes my hand and tells me to sit down. She scans my résumé, catching an item that makes her pause.

"Mr. Elwood," she says, smiling. "I see you've worked on the Hill."

I'm riding in a black SUV heading down First Street toward CNN Studios. Beside me sits Jon Powers, an army officer fresh off a tour in Iraq, and Michael Tucker, a filmmaker. "When you get on set, remember to emphasize that young audiences need to watch this film," I coach them. "Putting an R-rating on it is limiting the exact people who should see what war is like firsthand. The kids who might enlist."

Powers nods, mouthing my words to himself. I walk him through his talking points one more time as the SUV pulls up to the tan-and-glass building housing CNN's DC bureau.

"If this film gets rated R, it hurts the youth of America," I repeat when we step into the lobby and receive our security badges.

Powers is a subject of the documentary *Gunner Palace*, directed by Tucker, about soldiers living in Saddam Hussein's son Uday's pleasure palace during the second Iraq War. Venture has been tasked with keeping a PG-13 rating on a film in which the word *fuck* is uttered more than forty-two times. MPAA rules state if the word *fuck* is said in a movie more than once, the film receives an automatic R. And an R means fewer ticket sales.

It's my first PR campaign. My strategy has been to flood the zone. Make as much noise as we could. I've called television bookers and producers from a landline in Venture's basement office. "The Iraq War is a killing field right now," I spitballed. "Teenagers being recruited by the army need to see this film."

"I don't have time for this," beleaguered bookers said before hanging up.

"This isn't my beat," I heard again and again. "Take me off your list."

I'm twenty-four years old—my "save the children" pitch was born out of instinct. I didn't train in a press shop on the Hill. Venture has two other employees and pays me $35,000 a year, but my gut told me I was on to something. After a barrage of calls, I got through to a segment producer at CNN. In passing, I mentioned that Powers was from Buffalo, New York.

"Lucky break," the producer said. "Wolf Blitzer is from Buffalo. We'll help your guy out."

The CNN set is smaller than I imagined. The studio looks like a toy replica of what you see on-screen. The idea that this tiny room is responsible for so much influence seems incongruous, like ants carrying an apple. A line producer walks Powers from the green room to his mark. We have four minutes of camera time. Powers is calm. He has faced down RPG fire in Baghdad; he can handle a few questions from a cable news anchor.

I watch the segment on the TV in the green room, imagining the audience watching at home. Powers and Tucker stick to our script, repeating my talking points about the film educating America's youth about the harsh realities of war.

As the anchor nods like a concerned parent, I watch as Powers's words—*my* words—become legitimate in real time because he's saying them on cable news. In an instant, ideas I thought up in a windowless office appear to become reality, certified by CNN itself. The audience doesn't see me building the machine that creates this illusion. They don't even know I exist. If a PR person appears on TV, it usually means we've fucked up.

As CNN broadcasts my message to millions of Americans, I realize my job isn't to manipulate public opinion. My job is to get gatekeepers like CNN to do it for me. Once you have ink, your story becomes real. A conversation starts that didn't exist moments before, a conversation nobody would think to have if you hadn't started it. The public begins to accept something you created out of nothing.

And I have something reporters will always need: access to inside information. Information is the only commodity I control, but in this world it's valuable currency. The media demand constant fuel. I can feed information to reporters and toggle how much they see. I feel as if I've put on a pair of night-vision goggles that reveal the hidden machines powering the world. I begin to see levers I can pull. The adrenaline that spikes feels stronger than any line of cocaine.

The press pick up our message and run with it. We secure a sympathetic review by A. O. Scott in the *New York Times*. "The raw inconclusiveness of 'Gunner Palace' is the truest measure of its authenticity as an artifact of our time and of its value for future attempts to understand what the United States is doing in Iraq," he writes. Fox News's Sean Hannity and Alan Colmes bring on Powers for a five-minute segment. MSNBC also does a segment with Powers and the director. My first time out, I secure a cable news "hat trick."

A few weeks later, I attend the premiere of *Gunner Palace*. Sen. Ted Kennedy shows face on the red carpet. The house lights go down, and the screen lights up: "This film is rated PG-13."

I've just sunk a body.

Let me explain. I sank my first body when I was twelve. My father was the minister of an East Coast church, an easy walk to the ocean. Our house stood behind the church, and our front yard was the parish graveyard. Heavy metal bands tried to rent the property for record release parties. Aging, failing septic systems upstream yielded fecal counts in the hundreds of thousands in the creek running through the graveyard. A river of shit.

When a parishioner expired, I would get to spend time with my father, and I would be compensated for my time. Fifty dollars per body. All I had to do was hold the cross and look sad for an hour. Workers brought in earth-moving machines to dig the grave. When the casket was in place, we stacked flower pots between the hole and the bereaved.

During one burial, my father and I stood behind the flower pots. I could see down into the hole. "Yea though I walk through the valley of the shadow of death . . ." my father began. Then, over the mourners' bellowing, crying, and sniffling, I heard clods of earth falling and . . . *splashing*. Brown liquid was pooling up from the dark earth. I gave my father an elbow and nodded toward the bottom of the grave.

He picked up his pace. "I will fear no evil."

I watched shit-colored water swirl around the coffin. The coffin broke free from the dirt, floating, rising. I elbowed my father again.

"Steady the casket," he whispered.

Angling the cross just so, I was able to place one foot on terra firma and the other on today's Jane Doe.

"For thy rod and thy staff they comfort me."

By the closing prayer, my shoe was soaked through.

"Handle this. I'll be back soon," my father told me and then led the mourners to the parish hall. They were none the wiser. I worried that the coffin was going to float up and out of the hole. I was twelve, so I also worried that the body inside would come back to life. I jumped on the coffin, trying to submerge it. I slipped on its slick surface and fell into the grave.

It was the first time I helped create a false narrative. Cover up the truth when the wheels have fallen completely off the wagon. Remain calm and sink the body. The body is the truth. With *Gunner Palace*, the truth was that we wanted a PG-13 rating to sell more tickets. So, you sink the body. You make the public believe you want to keep vulnerable teenagers safe from the Iraq War. And with this body, I've made much more than fifty bucks.

I need to create this illusion again. All around me, I see power and more power. I'm low in DC's pecking order. Even Moynihan's aide Eric has more pull than me. But for the first time in my life, I've discovered a trick that makes people clap. A trick that I'm apparently good at. I need to master it. I need to see how far it can take me.

CHAPTER 2

Everyone Deserves Representation

I'm sweating through my best suit at the Garden Terrace at the Four Seasons in Georgetown. My table sits below a trellis of manicured ivy. Peter Brown is due to arrive in five minutes.

Earlier this afternoon, I got a call from a woman who said she was Peter Brown's assistant. "Can you meet Mr. Brown for a drink this afternoon?" she asked. "He's thinking about hiring you."

I agreed. Then I googled "Peter Brown."

Brown rose from running the record department at a store in Liverpool to managing the Beatles and sitting on the board of Apple Corps. He is mentioned by name in a Beatles song. He helps Robert De Niro promote the Tribeca Film Festival and takes Barbara Walters as his date to events. In the early 1980s, Brown moved to the PR game and now heads up Brown Lloyd James, a boutique firm based in New York.

Brown strides into the Garden Terrace wearing a tailored blue suit accented with a pink silk tie. His silver hair matches his cuff links. When we shake hands, he feels frail but somehow in charge of even this small physical interaction—which is incredibly disarming. A waiter materializes, asking, "Campari and soda, Mr. Brown?" I order a glass of Malbec. Our drinks arrive nearly instantaneously.

"So," I say, "tell me about the firm."

"Imagine Brown Lloyd James as a relationship brokerage," Brown says in an elegant English accent. "We solve ornate problems for extraordinary clients. Used to do it ages ago for John."

It takes me a moment to realize he's referring to John Lennon.

"John once called me in a pinch. He needed to get married immediately without the media hounding the ceremony. I found the one place on the bloody globe that fit the ticket. He and Yoko tied the knot in Gibraltar."

Coming out of a less remarkable man's mouth, this story would sound like shameless name-dropping. But Brown speaks softly, nonchalantly. He can afford to: Lennon canonized him in "The Ballad of John and Yoko": "Peter Brown called to say 'You can make it okay,'" Lennon sang. "'You can get married in Gibraltar, near Spain.'" A Beatle singing about your cocktail stories is better than being knighted. And Brown will later almost be knighted. The Crown will appoint him a Commander of the Order of the British Empire.

"My uncle Phil is a big Beatles fan," I say. "I'm named after him."

"John and Yoko bought an apartment in the building next to mine because they liked my view of Central Park. Yoko still lives there. Mick Jagger once sublet my apartment. When the term was up, he wouldn't give it back. We got into quite a dustup over it."

"Happens."

"We need someone in New York," Brown says. "To run a couple of accounts."

"What sort of accounts?"

"BLJ represents exotic clients. Countries. High-net-worth individuals."

Brown doesn't get specific, and I'm too impressed to pry. He isn't selling his firm. Rather, a new life that his demeanor telegraphs I'd be lucky to accept. I'm in the market for a new life. After Venture, I was hired away by the PR mega firm Burson-Marsteller. My biggest client was the U.S. Tuna Foundation, which tried to get pregnant women to eat, you guessed it, more tuna. We paid off academics to argue that a certain form of molecular mercury was too large to cross the blood–brain barrier. The National Healthy Mothers, Healthy Babies Coalition maintained that women of childbearing age should eat at least twelve ounces of seafood per week. We were caught by none other than the *New York Times*: "Industry Money Fans Debate on Fish," read the headline that exposed the whole nasty affair.

"Everyone deserves representation," Brown opines. "And anything is possible with the right amount of money."

"I have some references you can call."

Brown takes a slow sip of his Campari and soda. "What do I care what someone else thinks?"

"You need to sign this," Peter Brown's assistant tells me, sliding a form across the desk.

U.S. DEPARTMENT OF JUSTICE

REGISTRATION STATEMENT PURSUANT TO THE FOREIGN AGENTS REGISTRATION ACT OF 1938

List every foreign principal to whom you will render services:

Hassan Tatanaki, Great Socialist People's Libyan Arab Jamahiriya

I don't recognize the name "Tatanaki," but I sign the form without a second thought. I walk back out into the Brown Lloyd James offices. A dozen PR pros pace around gray laminate cubicles, firing pitches into phone lines. I hear conversations in Chinese and Arabic. I can't wait to get my hands dirty.

Peter Brown takes me to meet my new manager, BLJ's second-in-command and my direct boss. We go to lunch at Michael's, on West Fifty-Fifth Street, where we are ushered to the best table in the house. "Phil," Brown tells my new manager, "is our new operative."

Operative. The word lets me know I'm home.

PR firms employ two types of people: bureaucrats and operatives. Bureaucrats are the accountants. The conference call leaders. The digital paper pushers. Operatives infect newsrooms. Call reporters. Do whatever it takes to get ink. I have always been and will always be an operative. Put it on my tombstone.

Ninety percent of mega PR firms' staff are bureaucrats. These firms claim to be experts in media relations, adept at securing coverage. Most of them don't achieve results for their clients. They don't know how to start fires. They understand their job is to create paper. PowerPoint presentations. Spreadsheets. Revise website copy. At Burson-Marsteller, the weekly email we received with the roundup of coverage secured by the entire firm was embarrassing. Publicists pushed paper for years without placing a single story in a major paper.

But mega firms still charge clients millions for their services. It's a giant money suck. British conglomerate WPP earned £12.8 billion in 2021. But, hey, at least WPP's website has a charming tagline: "We use the power of creativity to build better futures for our people, planet, clients and communities." Here's a good rule of thumb: More jargon equals more bullshit. More bullshit equals more billable hours. More billable hours does not mean more coverage.

These firms don't know what to do with an operative. An operative at a mega firm is like a Navy SEAL working at the post office. During my tenure at Burson-Marsteller, I secured only one story, and not for lack of pitching. The bureaucrats shot down my wilder ideas, the ones that would actually have translated into coverage. They worried that by going after one client's enemies, they would anger another client. Or a potential client. By having such a large clientele, the megas ensure that all their clients get the most inoffensive, ineffective, and likely useless campaigns possible.

At Brown Lloyd James, I am hindered by no such constraints. Here, I can be myself. Here, I am among my own. (Okay, I stole those last two lines from *Thank You for Smoking*, a book I worshipped in high school. I imagine Nick Naylor would consider being plagiarized a professional honor.) Peter Brown has assembled a team comprised exclusively of operatives and has instructed them to start fires.

After Hurricane Katrina, one of BLJ's vice presidents arranged for the Qatari royal family to fly over New Orleans in Black Hawk helicopters to survey the devastation. Only after, of course, the Qataris pledged one hundred million dollars toward relief efforts. My manager has contacts in every newsroom from the *San Francisco Chronicle* to the *New York Times*. And then there's the interns. Just like on the Hill, they have a direct line to the elite.

Peter Brown moves through the world as a distinguished executive, with immaculately tailored suits fresh from Savile Row and a requirement that he sit in seat 1A when he must fly commercial. But he's a rock-and-roller at heart. Within weeks of my starting at the firm, Brown calls me and says, "Our client has a job for you. You're going to Chile. If you get into any trouble, I know the president."

"I hope I won't get into enough trouble that you have to call the president," I reply.

Forty-eight hours later, I'm riding above the streets of Santiago in a rickety cable car. In Chilean wineries, I source contacts for a nongovernmental organization that needs international voices to criticize a legislative proposal before the U.S. Congress. What feels like days later, I'm answering an email on a rooftop bar in Istanbul with a view of both the Hagia Sophia and the Blue Mosque. My once seldom-used passport is suddenly full of stamps.

Best of all, I convince Brown that I'm a more useful operative in DC than in New York. At BLJ's New York head-quarters, agents dress in Armani suits. I have two suits from Jos. A. Bank and prefer to work from my rooftop in cargo pants. I sign a lease on an apartment on Logan Circle, ten blocks from the White House.

The day I move in, I meander into a neighborhood bar called Commissary. It's discreet, and the drinks are cheap. I sit at the bar and order an old-fashioned. Commissary becomes my base of operations. It's the perfect hideout for lunches with *Wall Street Journal* scribes. *Politico* rarely "spots" people at Commissary.

I'm having breakfast at Commissary, sipping a mega mimosa, when an email comes through from one of BLJ's clients, a wealthy Turkish American industrialist. He's received intel that a Turkish barber named Sabri Bogday has been sentenced to death by religious authorities in Saudi Arabia for blasphemy. Bogday's crime? Someone getting a haircut overheard him say, "Goddamn it."

Get the English-speaking press to cover this, my client implores.

When you're trying to apply pressure through the press, you must know and exploit your enemies' weak spots. The Saudis don't have many. They are rich. They don't give a shit about political hits. But they don't like religious shame. So, it's time to play the shame game. The pitch writes itself: barbarism.

I call a DC friend and *Huffington Post* political blogger named Peter Slutsky. "The Saudis are going to kill this guy for saying 'goddamn it,'" I tell Slutsky. "Something we do every minute."

"Goddamn," Slutsky replies.

Slutsky and his twin brother Matthew write 750 words on Bogday's case. I win all 750 for my client. The piece is bleeding-heart perfection. "This situation is completely nuts and no reporters are stepping up to the plate to tell this man's story," the Slutskys write. "This case, and cases like it, have occurred and will continue to occur as long as international voices remain silent." The Slutskys also write in defense of a jailed Saudi Arabian blogger facing five years in prison for posting about the incident. I can use that. Reporters will come running to protect one of their own. I've got what I need: first ink. Once you create one moment out of nothing, you can create more. You have started a fire.

A few days later, Saudi Arabia is hosting a summit at the

United Nations to discuss, of all things, religious freedom. I send the *HuffPo* piece to reporters from Reuters and the *New York Times*. "If you want a story, get down to the UN and ask questions about Bogday," I tell them. "You've got a rare chance to confront a brutal regime about a religious prisoner."

At the summit, reporters pepper Saudi officials with probing questions. Caught off guard, the officials stumble over their answers. A week later, the Saudis buy Bogday a one-way ticket to Istanbul and tell him never to come back to their kingdom.

I celebrate over a few rounds with Peter Slutsky at Commissary. "Bogday owes this Jew free haircuts for life," he says, raising a glass.

He's so jovial, I try to match it. "The best part is he'll never know I exist," I say.

"Phil, we just saved a man's life," Slutsky says, suddenly serious. Suddenly proud.

Instead of feeling satisfaction, I am unsettled. Low when I should be riding a high. I think about my college therapist's diagnosis of "situational depression." But this heavy, shaky feeling follows me around regardless of the situation. There is a wide gap between how I should feel and how I actually do.

The next night, I go back to Commissary alone. Then the next. And then back the next day for a mega mimosa breakfast. When I'm low, it's easier to make small talk with reporters after I've had a few old-fashioneds. No matter how many stories I place, I still feel that something is wrong with me. Another drink, another joint. The bar tabs add up, then add up some more. Within six months of starting at BLJ I'm twenty grand in credit card debt.

Margarita likes to drink martinis at lunch. And after lunch. After a few extra-dirty ones at a dive bar in Hell's Kitchen, Margarita still looks poised in her tight red dress. She can still walk a straight line in her high heels. In my wingtips, I cannot.

I'm five rounds into one of Peter Brown's exotic assignments. I'm to escort Russia Today's editor in chief through New York's newsrooms and introduce her to Brown's contacts. Margarita Simonyan got the job at Russia Today at the ripe old age of twenty-five. She knows Vladimir Putin personally. In 2022, a State Department report will call her "adept at serving up lies as truths—and with a smile." Along with Al Jazeera, Russia Today is one of two foreign media entities represented by BLJ. Our goal is to legitimize it in the American news market.

In polls, the news media's popularity hovers around 10 percent, the same rating enjoyed by Congress and baby seal clubbers. The press need PR pros more than anyone. All the major networks have us flaks on staff in case of a crisis. A good friend of mine was one of CNN's PR people in 2004. One Friday, the storied program *Crossfire* booked a comedian as its guest. What could possibly go wrong? The comedian was Jon Stewart. The hosts of *Crossfire* that evening were Paul Begala and Tucker Carlson. In a now-infamous segment, Stewart ripped cable news to shreds on air, calling Carlson a "dick" and a "failure." And he looked like a hero for it. It was probably the worst day of my friend's career. She had to try to clear up the fiasco for Page Six and the other news-starved gossip columns that had pounced on the story. Whenever the news organization becomes the story, you are about to have a nightmare news cycle. Stewart caught lightning in a bottle: he got *Crossfire* canceled. I'm quite sure each host has his version of revisionist history, but in the Wikipedia entry for *Crossfire*, the heading "Jon Stewart's appearance" appears just before "Cancellation."

In New York, Simonyan and I use Brown's limitless Rolodex to careen through offices of the city's media luminaries. We end up, very drunk, at the office of the *Nation* with the magazine's publisher, Katrina vanden Heuvel. The *Nation* prides itself on being one of the country's most liberal publications. I have never been to a meeting of the Communist Party, but I imagine its talking points could have been generated from Simonyan and vanden Heuvel's back-and-forth.

Today, I'm acting as a double agent. Every reporter I introduce Simonyan to also becomes one of my contacts. Weeks later, I will ask vanden Heuvel for an introduction to a journalist at the *Nation*. She connects us immediately. If you make one friend inside a newsroom, you can get them to introduce you to their colleagues. You can infect that newsroom.

Back in DC, I continue my viral outbreak. I have drinks with a young new *Wall Street Journal* reporter. I feed her some intel. She invites me to a journalists' poker game. I build from one reporter to the next until I've got a network across the *Journal*. It's a slow process. But now, when I scan through my dozen contacts at the paper, I can trace them all back to my first meeting with the up-and-comer who liked to play poker.

Soon, my Rolodex of reporters balloons: Ken Vogel at *Politico*, Dan Wagner at the Associated Press, and Reuters bureau chiefs based in Istanbul and Ankara, who prove useful for my Turkish American client. When I call, they pick up. I can send a message to a well-respected reporter at any number of the top-tier journalism outfits and get a response from them in minutes. They know I have something juicy, an exclusive. They build their careers, and I do my job to spin a story for a client. I'm understanding better every day how influence works, and my own influence is growing.

Influence—*wasta* in Arabic—means many things to many people, but my life's work is best encapsulated by the word's seventeenth-century etymology: "unobservable forces that produce effects by insensible or invisible means." PR people like me hide in plain sight, influencing news coverage. Like most PR pros, I get journalists to tell stories about our clients or about our clients' enemies. These clients range from individuals to companies to entire countries, who pay, at a minimum, tens of thousands of dollars a month to engage our services. Sometimes hundreds of thousands a month.

Sounds innocent enough, right? Right.

My industry is worth approximately $129 billion. We will

do *anything* to earn those billions. The best journalists in the world aren't always breaking stories because of their dogged reporting skills; they're breaking them because they rely on people like me to feed them exclusive scoops. We use journalists to do our clients' bidding. And then the public reads their stories and believes them because they are coming from a trusted news source and not a corporate bagman.

Sadly, we have the journalists outnumbered. Three hundred thousand people are employed by the PR industry in the United States, compared to an estimated forty thousand journalists. There are seven and a half PR pros for every journalist. Would you take those odds in a fight? We also have journalists outgunned. The average salary for a PR professional is a multiple of what a journalist of comparable experience can make. And we have them on our side. They need us because we're a main source of information feeding today's nonstop hunger for media content. Media relations practitioners operate between the source and the journalist. We will always find a news outlet to make our clients' stories appear legitimate.

Seven hundred fifty words. That's how long your average print news story is. To manage their expectations, I tell my clients that we want to win 50.1% of a story. That's 376 words. That is what I am fighting for. "Congress shall make no law respecting an establishment of religion, or prohibiting the free exercise thereof; or abridging the freedom of speech, or of the press . . ." The first words of the First Amendment give me the rights I need to fight for my 376 words, my clients provide me with the resources. Sometimes you can game the system and get 80 or 90 percent of the story placed. Embargo dates, background and off-the-record conversations, access to clients, access to proprietary information, a look at a lawsuit before it's filed, an internal email from a CEO, a surreptitiously recorded Zoom call, an internal memo, or a full-fledged whistleblower—all are weapons in the arsenal that allows a person in my position to control where and when a news event will occur.

But calling the journalist would, normally, be starting in the middle of the story.

When I am trying to place a story, I plan for it to take at least a month. Twenty phone calls. In a 2024 world, I send hundreds of Signal messages. And only one or two emails. Email is the easiest to subpoena, so I limit my work over that platform. The process generally goes something like this. A client calls the firm and presents us with a problem. We do an intake call to understand the scope of the damage. I take the allowed incubation time to consider our options. This can range from thirty minutes in the worst case to a day or two in the best.

I am about to admit to a trade secret here, one that might piss off a few people: I engage in the equivalent of "insider trading" with the media on a regular basis. I don't just talk to myself during this period. I use a group of a dozen journalists to field-test ideas. During my incubation period, I'll call one or two of them and float a strategy by them that has not been given to the client. It's always positioned as "What if, hypothetically, my client decided to do X . . . Would that be newsworthy?" And I make sure that all these calls are off the record. I'm not sure what a journalism school ethics professor would think of this practice.

I then present the plan to an internal audience at the firm. Because what I come up with is normally a bit crazy, it then gets modified. After this, the firm presents the strategy to the client. Then we convince them to take our advice.

This is where a reporter would normally get involved. If we are lucky, I'll know a reporter who will take the story immediately. However, normally, I need to ask someone at the target publication for a recommendation of a reporter who covers the issue in question. For the most part, reporter friends will send an email introducing me to a colleague. I then switch the conversation to Signal as quickly as possible and send some version of the following message: "I have a piece of information that no one else has. Do you want it?" Generally, reporters will give you a call after that. Then you move into the "discovery" phase.

The discovery phase is when I spend my currency. I have never bribed a journalist. I have heard of it happening in other countries. Clients have asked me to do it. I have worked with a former foreign journalist who had a penchant for taking bribes. But I have never bribed one myself. When I refer to spending my currency, I mean the proprietary information my client has given me to dole out to the media. Once I no longer have any new information to give a journalist, I become irrelevant to the story. More important, I have lost all leverage in the conversation.

Remember, this conversation takes place over a month. I can add my own editorial spin at each point in the conversation. If my client's opponent is a rival company, I can (off the record) impugn its credibility to my heart's content. If the opponent is another country, I can pick any negative item from that country's daily news and send it to the reporter or reporters I am working with on the issue. I am a bug in their ear, and 95 percent of what I say never sees its way into print (thank God). But there is that pesky 5 percent. I'm paid to disseminate information. I tell the truth from a monetized point of view.

A few weeks before Christmas 2008, I get a call from my manager. "I have a draft op-ed I need you to take a look at," he says.

I open the attachment and read the byline: "Muammar Gaddafi."

The form I signed on my first day at BLJ tumbles out of my memory. The word *Libya* was right there in black and white. Our client Hassan Tatanaki is a surrogate for Colonel Gaddafi. I'd agreed to represent the dictator of Libya.

The form, called a Foreign Agents Registration Act (or FARA) Statement, exists only because of another dictator, Adolf Hitler. In 1933, Hitler wanted to create positive spin for Nazi Germany in the minds of U.S. citizens. How did he do it? He hired American PR firms. The firms pushed Nazi propaganda to the American public through op-eds in newspapers. Congress thought this was beyond the pale and, in 1938, passed an act requiring all firms working for foreign powers to register with the Department of Justice.

Foreign dictators hiring American PR firms is still common practice. Take Ketchum, a public relations outfit owned by the holding company Omnicom Group, one of the mega PR firms. Vladimir Putin's Russia was one of Ketchum's largest clients. From 2006 to 2015, one of America's greatest adversaries paid tens of millions in fees to an American public relations firm. In 2013, Ketchum placed an op-ed from Putin in the *New York Times* about the Syrian civil war. Ketchum also does work for the American government: the Department of Education, the Department of Health and Human Services, the Internal Revenue Service, and the U.S. Army. If you work for Russia, you should not have a U.S. government contract.

In 2004, Ketchum was accused of "covert propaganda" when it used actors to play journalists in videos shot for a client. In this case, the U.S. Government Accountability Office found the firm in violation of the federal propaganda ban. But Ketchum's campaigns have been awarded "Campaign of the Year" at least six times by *PRWeek*, so they've got that going for them.

And while we are telling tales out of school, let's have a look at one of my favorites: Qorvis. Qorvis has the distinction of being the go-to PR firm for the Kingdom of Saudi

Arabia. Shortly after the events of September 11, 2001, the kingdom hired Qorvis for a cool $14.7 million, paid between March and September 2002. One of the tactics deployed was to use an astroturf (or front) organization called the Alliance for Peace and Justice to run radio ads promoting Saudi messaging in the United States mere months after 9/11. When, in 2004, the FBI raided Qorvis's offices, the firm called the raid a "compliance inquiry" regarding the Foreign Agents Registration Act.

Inflation hit the kingdom after Jamal Khashoggi, a columnist for the *Washington Post*, was abducted, tortured, murdered, and dismembered on October 2, 2018, at the direction of the Saudi Arabian government. It cost the Saudis $18.8 million in PR cleanup fees for killing just one person. Qorvis gobbled that money up between October 2018 and July 2019.

Foreign governments hire American PR firms because they've seen how skillfully we protect American politicians and corporations. In October 2004, prior to New York State governor Eliot Spitzer's self-immolation, he looked into the American International Group (aka AIG), a massive finance and insurance company that in 2008 would need a significant bailout from the U.S. taxpayer for misbehavior. AIG did not care for the inquiry and hired Qorvis to ameliorate the situation. You know what's easier than crisis communications? Paying people off to say nice things about your client. Twenty-five-thousand-dollar retainers and ten-thousand-dollar television appearance fees were offered to former Securities and Exchange Commission (SEC) officials and think tank staffers. When they were caught, Qorvis called it "research." Qorvis perfected its bag of tricks with American conglomerates and then sold it to the Saudis for a multiple of the price. Not a bad business model.

At BLJ, we're in the same business. We prove our skills in DC and New York and then export the strategies to the highest foreign bidder.

Gaddafi's op-ed is a rambling, pro-Russia, anti–NATO expansion screed. I edit the piece, wordsmithing long-winded paragraphs into buzzy sound bites designed to catch an editor's attention. When placing an op-ed, you need to hit a specific audience. If you're pitching a conservative argument, you shoot for the *Wall Street Journal.* If you're pitching six hundred words of crazy from a North African dictator, you enlist a second-tier publication like the *Washington Times.*

I call up the latter's op-ed editor.

"You're full of shit," she says when I tell her my client's name.

I have to spend an hour convincing her I'm a legitimate representative of Libya's "Brother Leader."

A few days later, I pick up a copy of the *Washington Times* on my way to Commissary. The headline reads, "Gaddafi: Provoking Russia." I join a small group of people who can say their words have appeared under the byline "Muammar Gaddafi." I'm not sure if I'm proud of what I've pulled off or scared of what I'm capable of. It's unsettling, like watching someone get mugged in broad daylight and doing nothing to stop it.

At BLJ's Christmas party, Peter Brown asks me to come to his apartment an hour before the other guests. I'm awed by his views of Central Park, his double living rooms, and his museum-chic furniture. In one bathroom hang pictures of Peter with the Queen of England, Peter with John Lennon, Peter with Ronald Reagan. Every time someone uses his toilet, Brown lets them know he has access to influence. Linking undeniable impulses is part of his genius. He understands that everyone is seduced by fame and that everyone needs to defecate.

"Are you seeing anyone, Phil?" Brown asks when I join him beside his piano. It's his first hint at an interest in my personal life.

"Not at the moment," I say.

"Who's your favorite actress?"

I've recently watched *Layer Cake*, so I say Sienna Miller's not bad.

"She's a friend. I could introduce you."

"Maybe she's a little out of my league. But thanks for the offer."

A who's who of the media trickles through the door. Michael Elliott, the editor of *Time*, walks in with senior executives at the *Wall Street Journal*. Not far behind them are Barbara Walters, Yoko Ono, and Donald Trump.

"Don't shake Trump's hand. He's a germaphobe," Peter whispers in my ear.

I've invited my childhood friend Preston, an East Coast, elite university–educated investment banker. When I need the right-wing take on a PR campaign, I tap Preston. As he says, "Nobody who doesn't have a generator and two years' worth of food in their garage outflanks me to the right." I describe him as "authoritarian-curious."

When I call Preston for his take on a story, it's not unusual to find him cleaning his "wireless hole punchers," his loving nickname for his AR-15s. Plural. Punch a code into a keypad in his den, and a false bookcase swings open to reveal his gun locker, which is filled with short-barreled AR-15s, some loaded with .30-caliber subsonic rounds "almost as quiet as you see in the movies." Preston says he's big believer in the importance of "diversity," so he also has shotguns, pistols, and precision long-range rifles. The locker is stocked with more than enough ammunition to keep his suburban home, in one of the lowest-crime zip codes in the country, safe indefinitely from . . . no one exactly knows. Bonuses from Preston's current investment bank finance this arsenal. I've had friends arm themselves because they are worried there is going to be another civil war. Preston arms himself because he's *hoping* for a civil war.

"Al Jazeera had a birthday party for a terrorist live on air," I recently told Preston, crowd-testing ideas for the network to break into the American news market. "How do we get around that?"

"There is no getting around that in the American states," Preston replied.

"You mean the red states?"

"Said what I said. Just because you're a U.S. citizen, it doesn't mean you're an American. Americans aren't going to watch the Terrorist News Network."

"Fuck," I said.

"Barack Hussein Obama," Preston finished.

When Preston arrives at the party, he is mystified by a huge vase filled with bananas. He glowers at the cornucopia of public relations professionals, celebrities, and BLJ clients. "All the worst humans," he says, "gathered in one place."

"Play nice," I say.

I make small talk with Barbara Walters and watch Donald Trump avoid handshakes. I've heard Trump is showing face because he wants to ink deals with Gaddafi. Libya has a multibillion-dollar sovereign wealth fund. Peter Brown might be able to provide access. I grab another flute of champagne and overhear Preston berating a *New York Times* journalist.

"Your profession has disgraced itself," he says. "You people have no pride. No shame."

I sip my bubbly and spot Peter Brown across the room, making Barbara Walters laugh. Brown is completely comfortable with how the world works and his place in it. He understands the hidden machinery behind it all. He knows how to operate it. And he understands that the most important thing of all is how you look while you're doing it. How you appear. He once told me, "We can't just do a good job. We also have to *appear* to do a good job."

And that's public relations. If you can do that, then you can do whatever you want, and there won't be any consequences. You can represent a dictator, and everyone still comes to your Christmas party.

My cab heads across the underside of Foggy Bottom and stops in front of the Watergate Hotel. The driver hands me a blank receipt. Blank cab receipts are the joy of every expense-accounted staffer in DC. An eight-dollar cab ride can transform into a fifty-dollar trip to the airport. I go to the airport a lot.

The Watergate's exterior looks like ribbons flowing in the wind. Once a posh address, the Watergate is slowly dying. Bob Dole used to live here; now the highlight is the Safeway in the basement. DC's zone-based taxi fare system was influenced by Dole, who wanted to ensure that he could ride from his residence in the Watergate complex to his Senate office in a one-zone ride.

I'm stressed because Peter Brown called me an hour ago and said, "You need to get down to the Libyan embassy." Lately, Brown has developed a penchant for calling at all hours with orders. Orders to jump on the next plane out of town. Orders to put out a fire. Or to light a match.

"What happened?" I asked.

"Our client is very happy," Brown said. "But the world will be very displeased."

Inside the Watergate's office building, I head through a nondescript door into a suite full of Libyan flags and portraits of Muammar Gaddafi. The embassy's décor is tacky, stuck in the 1980s. Everything about the Gaddafis is stuck in the '80s—and covered in layers of cigarette smoke.

Ambassador Ali Suleiman Aujali invites me to sit down at an oval desk. Last time I was here, we had Donald Trump on speakerphone setting up a game of golf for the Libyan ambassador.

"I gotta ask. Why did you pick the Watergate?" I say once I'm seated.

"It was available," Aujali replies.

"I'd imagine," I say. "Nothing shady has ever happened here."

"Today is a great day for our country," Aujali says, beaming.

He fills me in. Tomorrow, Scotland will release Abdelbaset al-Megrahi, the terrorist responsible for the bombing of Pan Am Flight 103 over Lockerbie. Apparently because he has cancer and the Scots believe in compassion toward terrorists. Al-Megrahi is set to receive a hero's welcome back home in Libya.

"The Brother Leader doesn't want the press to spoil his moment of triumph," Aujali explains.

"Oh, they are going to try."

We're in a fiery-red space beyond crisis. The world will find out about al-Megrahi's release in less than twenty-four hours. Then comes the storm of negative coverage. Al-Megrahi murdered Americans. Men, women, children. A lot of them. There is nothing I can do to stop this runaway train. But I can create a counternarrative. I think it up before I leave the Watergate: *Libya is America's ally in the war on terror. We have bigger fish to fry than one asshole who blew up a plane in the eighties.* I need one story. One headline to say that there is some dissent in the international outcry against Libya. Anything counts.

Back at my apartment, I scan old Google Alerts for "Libya." Four members of Congress traveled there in 2004, before the United States restored diplomatic relations. They tried to open the door to the West. I smile when I see that one of them was Solomon Ortiz. I know Congressman Ortiz from a recent operation in Mexico. When an earthquake rocked Turkey in 1999, the Mexican government sent dogs trained to locate survivors in the rubble. Saved a lot of lives. After a flood hit Mexico's Tabasco region in 2007, BLJ's Turkish American client decided it was time to repay the debt and donated ambulances to the relief effort. Ortiz facilitated the transfer.

The next morning, the press begins. It's worse than I imagined. So bad that FBI director Robert S. Mueller pens an open letter to Scotland's cabinet secretary for justice. "Your action in releasing Megrahi is as inexplicable as it is detrimental to the cause of justice," he writes. "Indeed your action makes a mockery of the rule of law . . . You have given Megrahi a 'jubilant welcome' in Tripoli, according to the reporting. Where, I ask, is the justice?"

I give the news an hour to flood through DC before I

call Ortiz's office. "Listen, Libya is getting the shit kicked out of them in the media," I say to the staffer who answers the phone. "Your boss helped restore diplomatic ties so they won't sell C-Four and Semtex to anyone with fifty cents and a cause. You switched them to players in the war on terror. All this shitty press is going to push Libya away from us. We don't want them to undo all the good work your boss has done."

"I haven't hung up yet."

"I can draft an open letter. Ortiz can sign it."

"He'll consider it. That's the best I can do right now."

I dash off the letter: "Restoring diplomatic ties after such a prolonged period of animosity is not an easy process. There will be stumbling blocks on the road, but we should not be deterred from the course of peace and dialogue ... consider the years of hard work on behalf of both nations to build this relationship and to avoid undoing these efforts lightly." I throw on a suit, head up to the Hill, and drop off the letter at Ortiz's office. A few days later, it appears in my inbox, signed by the congressman. Not a word changed.

I ship the open letter off to Ken Vogel, an influence reporter at *Politico*. Once I've piqued Vogel's interest, I float him an invitation to a reception later that week at the Willard Hotel. BLJ is celebrating the fortieth anniversary of Muammar Gaddafi's rise to power. According to DC legend, the term *lobbying* was coined at the Willard during the presidency of Ulysses S. Grant. Seems like the appropriate venue for the occasion.

Nobody from any self-respecting nation attends the reception. So, the room is quite full. If North Korea had an ambassador, he'd be snacking on the cheese plate. I stand with Vogel at the bar, burrowing talking points into his ear.

"Congressman Ortiz wanted to be here," I spin. "But he had to attend Obama's address to the Joint Session of Congress."

Vogel's report on the party runs in *Politico* the next morning. The headline: "Knock Off the Libya-bashing, Ortiz Says." *Politico* prints whole chunks of my ghostwritten letter. A positive piece of press. Landed for the Gaddafis. Within weeks of al-Megrahi's release. I deserve whatever the opposite of a Pulitzer is.

I forward the article to Ambassador Aujali. "I'll pass it on to the Brother Leader," he says. "He will be pleased."

Peter Brown is also pleased. I get a ten-thousand-dollar-a-year raise. The extra money gets spent in bars instead of paying off my credit card debt.

I'm sleeping off a Commissary hangover when my phone rings.

"Get out of bed, pack a bag, and get in a cab," my manager's voice blares. "Your flight leaves for Vegas in an hour. I'll send you info via email."

I don't have time to ask questions. I've fastened my seat belt in coach before the email blips through on my BlackBerry. Subject: "Leaving Las Vegas." My stomach drops into my shoes as the boarding door closes. For the next three days, I'll be babysitting Muammar Gaddafi's son, and Libyan national security advisor, Mutassim Gaddafi at the Bellagio hotel.

CHAPTER 3

The Doctor and Las Vegas

FRIDAY

Ali lays out the rules for the weekend:

1. Don't look the Doctor in the eye.
2. Don't get in the Doctor's way.
3. Ever.
4. Call him the Doctor. Never Mutassim.

"Why does he insist on being called the Doctor?" I ask. "He doesn't have a medical degree, does he?"

"He has a degree in torture from Moscow State University," Ali replies.

Ali is the Doctor's head of security. He's a former professional soccer player whose hands are built like the heads of hammers. He looks like he could put me through a wall with his shoulder. We're sitting under chandelier light at Jasmine, a haute cuisine Chinese restaurant at the Bellagio. I'm drinking my calories, too nervous to stomach my obscenely priced sweet and sour pork. Outside the window, fountains dance in front of a half-size Eiffel Tower.

"You follow rules for your own safety. You understand?" Ali asks.

I jump in my velvet chair when a sharp burst of sound explodes from the Doctor's table a few feet away. False alarm. He's only popped another bottle of Moët. Long, stringy hair, sunken eyes, and cigarette ash–colored skin give Mutassim Gaddafi the look of an animated corpse. A brown velour suit hangs loose on his stick-thin frame.

His two-man entourage, both named "Muhammad," suck absently on lobster claws. Natasha, a model Mutassim flew in by private jet for the weekend, holds out her champagne flute and pouts her bright red lips. Mutassim's German personal trainer is also part of the crew, but I have yet to spot him. Maybe he's working out.

It's Friday night, the final days of Ramadan. Devout Muslims—which the Gaddafis claim to be—abstain from eating, drinking, smoking cigarettes, or having sex from sunup to sundown. Today I've seen the Doctor do three of those things. And I'll bet the house that Natasha wasn't flown in to tuck him into bed. You're definitely not supposed to spend Ramadan banging your infidel girlfriend and then heading to the pool for a noon cocktail.

The Doctor has never cared much for rules. I don't think a dictator's son even comprehends the concept. In his twenties, Mutassim plotted a coup against his father. This earned him points in the family, as Muammar had taken over Libya when *he* was in his twenties. So, the coup was more of a "coming of age"–type thing than a "something to kill your son for"–type thing, as the Doctor is now thirty-five and unexecuted. Quite the opposite: not only is he Muammar's national security advisor, but he leads his own army unit. This probably amounts to his playing dress-up in a military uniform for photo ops a few times a year.

The dinner bill comes to eight grand. I charge it to my company Amex. The nine suites on the twenty-ninth floor, rows of Cirque du Soleil tickets, and bottles of vintage bubbly all get racked up on this Amex. Peter Brown wants no record of this trip. No credit card bill emblazoned with the name "Gaddafi" leaked to the press by a Bellagio employee. This bacchanal must stay out of the news—a tough ask that requires I do the opposite of the thing at which I'm best.

I arrived in Vegas this morning with a thousand dollars in cash I'd borrowed from my friend Jon on the way to the airport and an email from the colleague I'm relieving of dictator duty. "Mutassim very well might be the next leader of the country. He's in Room 29601—only he goes in there," my colleague wrote. "Recent things that Mutassim has expressed interest in and that you may need to help line up for them: visiting the Harley-Davidson showroom, looking into buying a Cadillac Escalade with limo-style rear seats, buying a telescope, buying jean shorts (seriously), and seeing Cher perform on Saturday night (also seriously)."

My phone exploded before my cab passed Mandalay Bay. I answered to someone screaming at me in Arabic. I shouted back that I didn't speak Arabic. "Cleaning persons. They are telling us to leave the rooms. The Doctor still sleeping. Fix problem now." *Click*.

At the Bellagio, I found out the Doctor was threatening a housekeeper for trying to clean his suite. A few months prior, Mutassim's brother Hannibal was arrested at a Geneva hotel for beating a maid. Muammar Gaddafi retaliated by cutting oil supplies to Switzerland, yanking more than five billion in assets from Swiss banks, expelling Swiss diplomats, and detaining Swiss nationals in Libya. BLJ earned its bones cleaning up a slew of scathing headlines. We can't have another international scandal in Vegas. If Peter Brown opens the *New York Post* to the headline "Gaddafi Man-Child Tossed Out of Bellagio, Pisses in Fountain," I'm out of a job.

I sprinted to the concierge desk, where I caught the attention of a man in a periwinkle Armani suit. "As you can imagine," I said. "You and I have a bit of a problem."

"Oh, I don't have to use my imagination," he said. "It's quite tangible."

"We can all make it out of this alive if you tell Housekeeping to stay away from the following nine suites," I said.

I brokered a deal for the staff to clean Mutassim's suite only while he lounged in his cabana at the pool. I tipped the concierge a hundred bucks.

"There's more coming," I said. "I'm going to need a lot of help."

SATURDAY

A thousand glass flowers shimmer from the ceiling of the Bellagio's lobby. Harsh casino light bounces off a sculpture of a golden-hooved horse sequined into an equine disco ball. My fingers tap a jittery staccato against the marble concierge desk. The concierge scowls. I've just asked him to help me procure a large amount of cocaine. Twenty-four hours into the trip, he's already weary of the Doctor's demands. Five poolside cabanas. Front-row tickets to every show on the Strip. And now this.

The concierge scribbles a phone number on a slip of paper, passes it to me, and stalks away. I dial the drug dealer while walking past a bank of *Wheel of Fortune* slots.

"Room number?" a man's voice asks.

"Three-one-six-two-eight," I said, giving him the number for my own room.

"Leave a thousand dollars under a water glass on your bathroom sink."

I hang up, call Ali, and ask for a grand.

"Take it from my room," he says. "Closet."

I ride the elevator up to the twenty-ninth floor and unlock Suite 29603, Ali's suite. When I checked in, I found nine keycards fanned across my coffee table. A level of access I never asked for and don't want. His suite is twice the size of my hotel room. A bowl of fruit rots on a table made of gold-and-white stone. Ali is neat. These are an operative's quarters, not a party boy crash pad.

In a closet the size of my bedroom, I find three black

snakeskin briefcases. I click one open, revealing a nickel-plated 9mm Beretta and packets of hundred-dollar bills shrink-wrapped in ten-thousand-dollar increments. It's the most cash I've seen in my life, at least a million dollars.

I use a bundle of cash to scoot the handgun away, trying not to touch it. I rip open one of the bundles and peel off a thousand dollars. I hesitate, tempted. Three million dollars in this closet. Would Ali notice twenty grand missing? My credit card debt could go to zero. Then I look at the Beretta. My credit score won't mean much if I'm dead.

Back in my own room, I arrange the money under a water glass on the bathroom sink. It's a tight fit. I catch a glimpse of myself in a mirror set in front of an arrangement of white orchids. I've got raccoon circles under my eyes, I need a shave, and my suit begs almost audibly for a dry cleaner. A drug peddler for a dictator's entourage.

A Las Vegas area code calls my cell. Each member of the Libyan delegation has a burner phone. I've saved none of their numbers. I tell the voice on the other end where he can find the package, grab my laptop, and prop the door to my room open with the bolt lock.

At the private pool called the Cypress, I spot the Libyans lying out in the cabanas I reserved this morning at six. I collapse onto a chaise longue. The metal rods in my hip are on fire. I picture the three screws inside, the throbbing flesh around them. My hip aches when I'm tired, and I didn't sleep last night. After dinner, our entourage took a four-car motorcade to see the Cirque du Soleil. Best seats in the house. We left halfway through because the Doctor got bored and wanted to hit the casino. He spun the roulette wheel until past midnight while I fielded angry emails from BLJ's accountant.

At the pool bar, I buy a screwdriver to anesthetize the fire ants in my hip and call Preston. For the rest of the trip, I'll have a drink in my hand whenever I am standing still. A screwdriver in the morning hours, wine with lunch, vodka sodas after dinner, and bourbon to close out the evening. I'm glad we have a fleet of drivers.

"I'm babysitting the Gaddafi kid in Vegas," I tell Preston. "I'm freaking out. They have guns. And a few eight balls of cocaine. Well, in a few minutes they will."

"What kind of guns?" Preston asks, genuinely interested.

"A nine-millimeter."

"Never let anyone tell you Americans don't use the metric system. We measure our bullets in millimeters and our drugs in grams. Was the barrel threaded?" he asks.

"I have no fucking idea," I yell, trying to drink the ice in my empty highball glass. "I'm more worried they'll decide to shoot me with it."

"You need to get the hell out of Dodge," Preston says.

"I can't leave," I say. "They're giant children. They can't be left unsupervised."

"I'm serious, Phil. Just take off. A Gaddafi could shoot you in a hotel room, and the whole thing would be covered up."

"I know," I say. "I'm one of the people who'd help cover it up."

An hour later, someone has taken the cash, and the cocaine I hope was left in its place, from my room. I lie down on the linen bedspread, elevating my throbbing thigh onto a pillow. But there's no rest for those who help the wicked. I'm needed at the high-roller lounge. The Libyans arrived straight from the pool wearing robes and sandals and are being denied entry.

"We have a dress code," the pit boss explains to me when I arrive downstairs.

The Doctor screams in Arabic. He gives Ali a look that asks, *Is this a person we can hit?*

Ali shakes his head.

"Please," I plead. "Could you just put some shoes on?"

"No," the Doctor says.

I realize it's the first time he has spoken to me. I'm the help, and the help should be neither seen nor heard.

The Doctor reaches into the pocket of his robe and yanks out a package of stiff bills. It's enough to buy a Toyota Camry—and the magic number to make the pit boss stand down. In the high-roller lounge, I watch the Doctor lose the equivalent of my monthly income on one hand of blackjack. After a few more bad bets, he's down ninety-five grand, my annual salary at BLJ. Ali lights a Marlboro for him and beckons me with his index finger.

"The Doctor wants you to arrange a private jet for tomorrow," he says. "To take Natasha back to L.A."

I duck out to the sportsbook and call BLJ's preferred charter jet service. The charter company sends an invoice for six thousand dollars to my BlackBerry. I forward it to BLJ for approval. In response, I receive back the invoice I sent yesterday for the motorcade. A new quote has been attached. I'm instructed to print it out for the Libyans in black and white, to account for any color damage that took place during its printing and scanning back at BLJ. "Color damage" is lazy code for "doctoring." Sure enough, the firm has upped the original cost by twenty thousand. Markups are a common practice at PR firms. They are written into contracts. The standard is 17.5 percent on top of any expenses incurred on behalf of the client. I'm no mathematician, but this blows several miles past 17.5 percent.

Panicking, I call my colleague. "The only person I know of who has stolen from the Libyans was Doc Brown in *Back to the Future*, and that ended very badly for him," I tell him.

"Get it in cash," I'm instructed.

I print out the invoice at the concierge desk, in black and white. Glancing at it, you can barely tell BLJ has fudged the numbers. But when I look hard enough, I spot the Wite-Out at the edges of the numerals. Back at the high-roller lounge, I hand Ali the invoice.

"We'd prefer you paid in cash," I say.

"We'll take care of it tomorrow," he says. "Now the Doctor wants to go shopping."

The Doctor really does want jean shorts. And a Harley-Davidson. And to see Cher. We take our four-vehicle motorcade to the Venetian, where I shepherd the Libyans through the Grand Canal Shoppes. The Libyans are dressed in multicolored Adidas tracksuits. The Muhammad twins try to smoke in the Burberry store. I find the Doctor a pair of jorts at the Gap. On the floor of the Harley showroom, the Doctor berates a clerk after issues arise with shipping a pair of chrome choppers to Libya.

That night at the Colosseum, Cher commands the stage wearing a headdress made of golden feathers crowned by a snake. I'm sitting next to Ali, behind the Doctor and Natasha. The Doctor remains stone-faced through Cher's lung-busting rendition of "Gypsies, Tramps, and Thieves." For twenty years, Libya was a terrorist pariah state. You'd think the Doctor's first trip to Las Vegas would be exciting, but nothing impresses him. I guess because people aren't getting shot on the stage. He is incapable of joy.

Halfway through the show, I turn to Ali. He's conked out. His chest rises and falls, his exhalations fluttering his nose hairs. Staring at his drained, gray face, I feel something approaching empathy. I've been babysitting the Doctor for less than forty-eight hours, and I've already had enough. This is Ali's life day in and day out. He must be terrified all the time.

We leave before the curtain falls and head for the MGM Grand. The Strip is thick with Saturday night traffic. This, too, draws the Doctor's ire. He doesn't understand why the motorcade can't go lights and sirens through Vegas.

Another casino, another roulette table. No clocks. Two days of fluorescent lights, buffet advertisements, Marlboro smoke, and slot machine noise have merged into one nightmare memory, like a moving hellscape by Hieronymus Bosch. Natasha pouts, bored by watching the Doctor lose more money.

"Can we go to TAO now?" she whines. "You said we could go to TAO."

The words are hardly out of her mouth when the Doctor beelines for the exit. I limp after him, dialing our drivers. The motorcade must be waiting to ferry him from whim to whim. My cell doesn't connect in the casino. As I follow the Doctor past the MGM Grand's Garden Arena, a wash of humans hits the casino floor. The final bell has rung at the Mayweather vs. Márquez fight. Thirteen thousand people head for the exits. The crush separates the Doctor and me from the rest of the group. I chase him, my hip a ball of pain.

Outside, taxis clog the valet stand. Our motorcade is not among them. The Doctor releases a wail. He throws his hands up in the air and jumps up and down like a toddler who's been told it's his bedtime. Then he pauses, sucking air.

Please let it be over.

No, he's just lighting another Marlboro before resuming his tirade, smoke pouring out of his mouth. A man wearing a T-shirt reading "Kiss My Ace" gawks at this madman in a tracksuit. So do two women wearing nothing but thongs and American flag body paint.

I dial the driver over and over. Finally, he pulls up, and I get the Doctor into the SUV. The rest of the entourage appears and piles in.

At TAO, we cut the line. A bouncer stops Natasha at the VIP entrance. She's doesn't have ID. The Doctor rears back a fist, snarling. I jump in front of the bouncer, the headlines running through my brain.

"If you're going to hit anyone, hit me," I plead.

The Doctor cracks his first smile of the trip, as if that would give him a joy Vegas can't provide. Ali convinces him to return to the roulette wheel at the Bellagio. There, he pisses his country's money away on ten-thousand-dollar bets. As his stack of chips shrinks, the Doctor curses in Arabic.

"Get more cash from his room," Ali whispers to me. "He'll be angry if he runs out. It's in the closet."

"How much?"

"A bagful."

So, we're measuring money in bags now.

The Doctor's suite goes on forever and smells like mall cologne and chain-smoked Marlboros. The room is trashed. The housekeepers are as terrified of Mutassim as I am. I grab the plastic liner from the empty garbage can and enter the closet. I open a snakeskin briefcase and chuck money into the bag until it feels heavy. PR people are often disdainfully called bagmen. Tonight, the moniker is well earned.

Back down in the casino, the Doctor is screaming at the dealer. He's out of chips. Bundles from the garbage bag refill his stack. He sparks a Marlboro, pacified for the moment.

A cocktail waitress taps me on the shoulder, demanding that I pay eight dollars for my vodka soda. I do a double take. My group is spending hundreds of thousands of dollars in the hotel, and I must reach into my pocket for a comped drink.

SUNDAY

I wake to an email from BLJ's accountant. "What are you doing?" she writes. "This is madness!" Amex has been calling hourly, saying we've hit our credit limit. Peter Brown's Black Card doesn't have a limit. I don't want to imagine the bill we've racked up. And I haven't even paid the Bellagio for the flight of suites.

Another email sits in my inbox. Attached is an approved invoice for Natasha's private flight. I notice that the original $6,000 has been changed to $16,597.45. I read through the chain of emails.

> *BLJ Agent 1: Do your thing :)*
> *BLJ Agent 2: Just confirming—$16,597.45, right?*
> *BLJ Agent 1: Yes. Can you play w the fees to make*
>   *them add up to that?*

I print out the doctored invoice at the concierge desk. "Checking out today, sir?" the concierge asks.

"Yes, thank God."

"Indeed."

At the casino, I hand the invoice to Ali. He glances at it.

"That's sixty thousand total now," I tell him. "We'd like to be paid before you leave."

"Get the money from my room."

Up in his suite, I open the black snakeskin briefcase one more time. The cash is there. The handgun isn't. I wonder if Ali will shoot me with it if he discovers my theft. Or maybe the Doctor will put his degree in torture to good use. I remove six packages of ten-thousand-dollar bills. Just yesterday, I was worried about stealing twenty grand. BLJ has no such concerns.

I stash the sixty grand in my room safe. Guns stay on my mind. One day, I'll inherit a Smith and Wesson .38—a gun that comes come with a free lesson in public relations. It was the 1930s, and a man named George walked down the street of a small town in the Midwest. George heard the town drunk beating his wife, a woman named Mary. George rang their doorbell, the drunk answered the door, and George shot him dead with his Smith and Wesson .38 and then turned himself in to the police. But this particular midwestern town was occupied by a thousand souls. They looked after one another. There was no murder trial. George married Mary, and they remained happily married for sixty years. In the late 1960s, George gave the murder weapon to my grandfather, who willed it to my mother.

During media training, PR operatives learn that every

story has three parts: a villain, a victim, and a vindicator. In this story, Mary was the victim, and when he murdered the drunk, George became the villain. In the PR business, we try to convert a villain into a vindicator or a victim as fast as possible. And that's exactly what the town did when they found George "not guilty" sans trial. They made him the hero, a vindicator of battered women. The deceased drunk was switched from a murder victim to a wife beater who deserved to die. A villain. Every story needs a villain. Show me a good story without one.

But these are just stories. Midwestern tales. Ink in newspapers. I've got a real villain blowing smoke in my face. And I'd really like to avoid becoming the victim. The Gaddafis have enough money to make the Doctor the vindicator, even if he kills me. BLJ did it for the Doctor's brother Hannibal after he tortured that poor housekeeper. Come to think of it, we've also done it for Mutassim. After a rough few months of press, a photo op was set up with Secretary of State Hillary Clinton.

I turn all this over in my mind as I drink another screwdriver. But what I'm really wishing is that I had George's Smith and Wesson .38 tucked into my belt.

The motorcade ferries us toward Vegas's private airstrip. I'm in the lead car, up front with the driver. We're two miles away. Natasha's plane needs to be there. We've triple charged them for it.

I should confess that I am partially responsible for the

high cost of airfare for more than just the Gaddafi family. I once worked on behalf of the private jet owners of America. The job was to beat the airlines in a legislative fight over who would pay for the Federal Aviation Administration to modernize the air traffic control system. The private jet owners did not want to pay a user fee to land and take off. The proposed fee was twenty-five dollars. For perspective: a private jet burns twenty-five dollars of fuel in about one nanosecond. The airlines hired the best lobbying and PR firms to demonize the private jet owners. My job? Hit the airlines hard. As hearings on the issue were making their way through the House and Senate, I worked with an investigative reporter for the Associated Press. "What the airline industry wants from Washington it often gets, and no wonder," read the lede of her piece. "The people who regulate airlines on one day can become company executives the next—and the other way around." It's some of my finest early work. Peter Brown thought so, too. In short, we won. And now you, the passenger, pay a bit more so that the wealthy who fly on private planes can avoid a twenty-five-dollar fee.

I'm sorry.

At the airstrip, a Gulfstream jet and a smaller charter plane wait on the tarmac. I sprint into the office and hug the pilot. The Doctor poses for a picture with Natasha. Ali snaps a shot of their awkward hug. Their bodies do not really touch. They do not kiss goodbye. Natasha gets on her plane, and the Doctor boards his jet with the Muhammads in tow.

Ali is the last to board. I watch him climb the airstair.

Ten steps to go. Now two. He stops at the cabin door. Looks back at me.

"Aren't you riding back with us to New York?"

"My luggage is back at the hotel," I say.

I stare at the horizon until their plane disappears into the blue. I am exhausted. I can barely walk. But Ali and his gun are gone.

I take a surreal solo ride in the four-car motorcade back down the Strip. I think of the sixty grand in my hotel room safe. How much cash can you legally fly with on a domestic flight? I'm not sure. I text one of my colleagues at BLJ, asking if sixty grand will trip security.

"Strap that shit to your body," they reply.

I ask the driver to let me out on the corner of Flamingo Road and Las Vegas Boulevard. I limp into a massive CVS and purchase a roll of medical tape for four dollars and ten cents. I pay in cash, worried my BLJ Amex will finally scream uncle.

Up in my room, I secure the sixty grand along my rib cage. It bulges when I button my shirt. Adding a blazer helps. I feel like a drug runner.

The bill. Oh holy hell, the bill. Down at the front desk, I'm handed a stack of paper as thick as a Russian novel. My credit card is declined. The Doctor might be gone, but I'm still terrified, unsure of what they do to you in Vegas when you can't pay your seven-figure bill. I spend the next hour pacing around the bar next to the checkout desk while BLJ's accountant negotiates with Amex to increase my credit limit.

My card finally runs, and I head for the valet station. I'm almost outside, almost free, when I realize what I've forgotten. I turn around and head back to the desk, where I'm greeted by the concierge's familiar frowning face.

"Will there be anything more, sir?" he asks.

"I need a first-class ticket out of here."

When I walk into McCarran International, I remember that the three titanium rods in my leg set off metal detectors. How to spin the sixty thousand dollars taped to my body? I walk through the metal detector. The silence from that machine is the most golden sonic event of my life.

Just before the plane's doors close, Flavor Flav stumbles into the seat across the aisle from mine, with a giant clock hanging from his neck. He's very drunk and holding a ring of keys so large he's forced to put them into the overhead compartment.

"The Mayweather fight was money!" he screams, as a flight attendant buckles his seat belt. "I'm headed for New York, boiii."

Unfortunately, so am I. After three days of babysitting the homicidal son of a homicidal father, I just want to go home. But I can't. I'm flying a red-eye direct to New York. Muammar Gaddafi is en route to make his first speech to the United Nations General Assembly.

CHAPTER 4

No Fingerprints

In a yellow cab from JFK, I peel the sixty grand from my rib cage. The medical tape leaves raised red lines on my skin. Before I stuff the money into my backpack, I skim a thousand dollars from one of the stacks and tuck it into my wallet. I need to repay the friend who lent me cash for Vegas. Given the circumstances, I feel I'm being more than restrained with BLJ's stolen money.

The cab dumps me in front of BLJ's offices on West Fifty-Seventh Street. Upstairs, the office hums with activity, and I remember it is Monday morning. I find Peter Brown seated in his corner office contemplating the view of Columbus Circle. Brown's desk is tidy, not one silver pen out of place. I take the Libyans' cash out of the backpack and place it before him. Brown glances down at the pile, then up at my rumpled suit, my wild hair, my bloodshot eyes. Flavor Flav was rather boisterous on the red-eye. I had no choice but to drown him out with vodka sodas.

"Peter, I don't know what the hell just went on in Vegas," I say. "It was just, you know . . . They didn't like Cher . . . They had guns . . ." I haven't slept in three days. I'm aware that I'm not making much sense.

Brown looks annoyed and holds up a finger. "Why would I want to know about any of that?" he asks, sliding the money into a drawer.

"The whole trip was just so fucked up."

"But there were no news articles published about it," Brown says. "And that was your job."

The same cannot be said for Muammar Gaddafi's arrival in New York. For the New York media, Gaddafi's coming to town is something akin to both Christmas morning and a blood orgy. The next morning, Tuesday, BLJ's staff fields hundreds of press requests. The whole world is calling the office. And they have questions, so many questions.

Gaddafi's appearance before the UN General Assembly is what, in public relations, we call an inflection point. In *Back to the Future Part II*, Doc Brown uses a chalkboard to explain how a small event in the past can skew a time line, creating an alternative future. In public relations, we try to create alternative futures for our clients. We do this by capitalizing on an inflection point, a critical moment when the time line can skew toward, we hope, the positive. Gaddafi's televised speech in front of world leaders has the potential to erase decades of bad press and negative public perception. If you manage the coverage right, you can serve up rehabilitation, goodwill, and a new image, all in a single news cycle. And the public will eat it up with a spoon. If a client is redeemed in the eyes of both Fox News and CNN, it's as good as washing them in holy water.

Emerge, my client, reborn and rebranded—until the next scandal.

Every client, large and small, faces an inflection point. Some you create. Some are created for you. An inflection point usually comes after your client has shit the bed. Personally, I consider every crisis a golden opportunity. If my client lights their house on fire, you can be damn sure I'll get the press to blame outdated fire codes. I tell clients, "Don't be a hero. Always work to find a better villain."

Inflection points can go sideways, though. In 2000, British Petroleum sought to create an inflection point with a rebranding for the new millennium. The corporation paid PR firm Ogilvy and Mather $200 million to take it "Beyond Petroleum." The campaign was truly ambitious—and by "ambitious," I mean a complete departure from the truth. Let's look at the investments. In 1999, BP invested $45 million to buy Solarex, one of its largest bets on renewable energy. But that same year, it also invested billions of dollars in expanding its drilling both onshore and off. Its new slogan thus highlighted a minuscule portion of its overall energy portfolio while completely ignoring that the majority of the portfolio even existed. The unbridled cynicism it took to conceive this campaign is nearly unmatched in the modern era.

In March 2006, facts got in the way of BP's rebrand when about 267,000 gallons of its oil spilled into Alaska's Prudhoe Bay over the course of about five days. It was the largest spill on record on Alaska's North Slope—to date. In 2007, BP paid a criminal fine of $20 million, and in 2011, a civil penalty of $25 million.

I just want my life back. Six words I would have advised Tony Hayward never to say.

On April 20, 2010, an immense offshore rig operated by BP, known as the Deepwater Horizon, failed explosively, killing eleven people and becoming the source of the largest oil spill in U.S. history. Hayward, the CEO of Beyond Petroleum—who, incidentally, grew up in Slough, the town where the original, British version of *The Office* is set—was chased by a group of reporters in the days following the disaster. In response to a flurry of questions, Hayward reached into his rhetorical toolbox and came out with something truly worthy of the American *Office*'s "Michael Scott": "I just want my life back."

He resigned shortly thereafter.

In 2012, the State of Alaska would collect another $225 million from BP as a result of the Prudhoe Bay spill. That same year, BP would plead guilty to fourteen criminal counts related to the Deepwater Horizon disaster and pay fines of over $4.5 billion. Adding in the cost of subsequent private claims, and

Deepwater Horizon will eventually cost BP more than $65 billion. For BP, there is no moving "Beyond Petroleum."

Now our job is to make sure Gaddafi's inflection point doesn't attain a similar terminal velocity. Gaddafi wants his UN speech to skew his time line. He has spent decades as a global pariah, scarlet-lettered by President Ronald Reagan as the "Mad Dog of the Middle East." But in 2006, the United States restored full diplomatic ties with Libya. Then–Secretary of State Condoleezza Rice even visited the country. Gaddafi sees his UN General Assembly speech as an opportunity for rapprochement with the West. He's been offered a seat at the table. He wants to be welcomed with open arms as both a leader and a revolutionary.

Gaddafi's been in town less than twenty-four hours, and he's already gotten more ink than Iran's Mahmoud Ahmadinejad. And not the ink we want. The release of the mastermind behind the 1988 bombing of Pan Am Flight 103 over Lockerbie, Scotland, has angered world leaders. And the protesters currently on the streets of New York. New Jersey lost thirty-eight New Jerseyans in the attack. Media-savvy rabbi Shmuley Boteach has plans to mobilize the Jewish community to demonstrate outside the UN building.

And then there's the tent: BLJ has an entire team devoted to cleaning up the tent debacle.

For weeks, Gaddafi's aides have been trying to find a place to pitch the Brother Leader's massive Bedouin tent. The tent is a dick-waving flag that Gaddafi plants while on diplomatic missions. Call it a dictator's quirk—like the

Revolutionary Nuns, his cadre of four hundred beautiful female bodyguards trained in martial arts. Gaddafi
requested that he be able to erect the tent in the middle of
Central Park. Hard "no" from New York City. Then Engle-
wood, New Jersey, turned him down. When luxury hotels
slammed their doors in his face, the Libyans got desperate.
ABC News reported that Gaddafi aides had posed as members of the Netherlands' UN delegation to try to rent a town
house. "I'm not a linguist, but it became pretty clear I wasn't
dealing with the Dutch," the rental broker told ABC.

To the delight of the tabloids, the Bedouin tent has finally
found a home on Donald Trump's estate in Bedford, forty
miles north of New York City. This morning, an ABC News
helicopter flew over the property, photographing the tent
compound: satellite dishes, ornate rugs, and wall hangings
decorated with tiny camels. New York Democratic representative John Hall told the press, "This sponsor of terror is not
welcome here," and asked Secretary of State Hillary Clinton
to do "everything in your power" to send Gaddafi packing.
Quite an arrival in the very city where Pan Am Flight 103
was scheduled to land. Two hundred seventy dead. And this
dictator can't understand why they won't let him pitch a tent
in Central Park?

More bad news breaks while I'm in the office. Trump's
people speak to the press, denying that Donald Trump knew
Gaddafi was renting his estate. Peter Brown gets Trump on
the line minutes after the quote goes live. I linger outside the
door of Peter's office, listening in.

"Goddamn it," Brown nearly yells. "You knew exactly who the fuck you were renting it to." It's the loudest I've ever heard him raise his voice.

After a long day drinking from a fire hose of media requests, BLJ's staff head to a dive bar for a much-needed happy hour. We slide into a long booth, eyeing the bottles of amber booze behind the bar. Everyone orders a double.

"It's been one thing and then the next," one of BLJ's vice presidents laments. "First Gaddafi's limo wasn't RPG-proof. As if anyone has a fucking rocket launcher in Manhattan. Then we had to bring a goat to the Bedouin tent. In case they want to, you know, slaughter it. Our interns are feeding the goat."

"Do we even pay them?"

"Our accountant is flipping her shit," another staffer adds, holding a cocktail glass against his forehead like an ice pack. "The Libyan delegations have rented floors of suites at the Plaza. They're flying the Libyan flag on Fifth Avenue. Right next to the Israeli flag."

"Just be thankful Page Six hasn't discovered that little detail," I say.

"Yet."

"I just feel so bad for that poor goat," the VP says.

"Another round in the goat's honor?" I suggest.

"You know what's sad," the VP says, looking down into the ice melting at the bottom of her glass. "After all this, Gaddafi is sleeping alone at the Libyan Mission. In a tiny room. On a cot."

"Well," I say. "Let's hope the Brother Leader's speech goes well tomorrow."

"We are ready to hand out weapons to a million, or two million or three million, and another Vietnam will begin," Muammar Gaddafi warns the United Nations. He stands on the dais in a flowing brown robe, a massive black brooch in the shape of Africa pinned to his chest. "It doesn't matter to us. We no longer care about anything."

I'm watching Gaddafi's speech on a flat-screen TV in a suite at the Plaza. The lavish space is crammed with BLJ staff and thirty members of the Libyan delegation. Everyone sips from their own personal bottle of Veuve Clicquot. Libyan children scurry around the Oriental vases and jump up and down upon the velvet sofas. Across the room, the Doctor cheers and chugs from his bottle.

I flinched earlier, when the Doctor walked into the suite flanked by Ali. The fear I had felt in Vegas bubbled up in my throat. It's a hot, sick feeling. A feeling not even half a bottle of Veuve can wash away. When I saw him, I darted to the far end of the room, hiding out with the kids, hoping the Doctor wouldn't catch sight of me.

When his father promises the gathered world leaders that he'll put his finger in the eyes of those who doubt that Libya is ruled by anyone other than its people, the Doctor calls for a toast. BLJ's staff and the Libyans raise their bottles. I clink bottles with a Libyan delegate smoking a cigar as Gaddafi suggests the UN headquarters be relocated to Libya, so he can avoid jet lag. This speech went off the rails when Gaddafi was introduced as "Leader of the Revolution of the Socialist People's Libyan Arab Jamahiriya, President of the African Union, and King of African Kings." Scheduled to speak for fifteen minutes, Gaddafi has been rambling for nearly an hour. He demands $7.77 trillion as reparation for colonial crimes in Africa. He rips a page from a copy of the United Nations Charter and tosses it into the air behind him. The viewing party at the Plaza nod and smile idiotically, as if we're proud parents at a child's ballet recital.

When Gaddafi calls for Israel and Palestine to be merged into a joint state called "Isratine," I can stand it no longer. I sneak out of the suite before the "Brother Leader and Guide of the Revolution" concludes his remarks. Outside, I hit Fifth Avenue, buy a pack of Camels, fire one up, and start walking south without a destination in mind. Four blocks later, my hip catches fire. I hail a cab and tell the driver to take me to Penn Station.

I board an Amtrak back to DC. I have a fear hangover. Over the next forty-eight hours, my phone explodes with panicked dispatches from the BLJ team in New York. Gaddafi went on *Larry King Live*. King welcomed him by accidentally calling him *"Muhammad* Gaddafi." Though he speaks English, Gaddafi insisted on using an interpreter. When King asked Gaddafi what his first impressions of America were, he replied, "Nothing." He called the UN Charter worthless. King will later tell interviewer Piers Morgan, "As a dictator, he's among the worst. As an interview, he is the worst." Morgan wonders what drugs Gaddafi took before his General Assembly speech.

We get all the wrong headlines. Gaddafi wanted to march into New York as a triumphant leader, ready to take his place on the world stage. He leaves an international joke. Worse, his carefully constructed image is demystified. For forty years, Gaddafi ruled as a feared dictator who—rumor had it—took pleasure in personally executing whomever he pleased. BLJ tried to keep it that way. But a PR firm can do only so much. What do you do with a client who calls for getting rid of Switzerland? Who doesn't like Switzerland? I've never had a client this uncontrollable, a caricature of a dictator who is so evil it's almost funny. And I never will again. Unless Kim Jong Un decides to hire me.

Gaddafi's inflection point has gone sideways in spectacular fashion. His time line has skewed into the wrong alternative future, maybe forever. I think about the goat wandering around the Bedouin tent. I wonder if it survived. An odd saying, one of Preston's, comes to mind: "You can't unfuck a goat."

I spend the next few months trying to unfuck this goat.

In April, I get an email from an agent at the counterespionage division at the Department of Justice. They want to go through BLJ's files to ensure we're in compliance with the Foreign Agents Registration Act. I know we're not. Peter Brown has told me not to file FARA forms for the Libyans.

When the agents visit our New York office, our interns

serve them tea. The agents give me two options: one, lay out all the files for them to review or, two, they will search our file cabinets. I choose option one and lay out all the FARA filings. I don't show them anything about the Gaddafis.

At Dulles International, I meet three American reporters at security. I always meet reporters before the security checkpoints in case a border agent doesn't accept their visa. Most security personnel have never seen a Libyan visa, which these reporters all have courtesy of me. At the very least, it raises eyebrows. Today, I have to call the Libyan embassy and put someone there on the phone with the gate agent.

"Let them through," the embassy tells them. "The trip is sanctioned by the Brother Leader."

We proceed directly to a bar. "Headed someplace we can't drink for a while," says Matt Labash of the *Weekly Standard*. "Might as well get it in now."

The reporters are all kinds of curious about the work BLJ is doing for Gaddafi.

"If you run into Mutassim, watch your back" is all I'll say.

I'm sending these reporters to a "terrorist rehabilitation camp" in Tripoli, Libya's capital. There, they'll meet Islamic fundamentalist terrorists who have changed their murderous ways, put down their Kalashnikovs and truck bombs, and who now study a reformed text of jihad called *The Book of Correctional Studies*. This is a propaganda tour for Saif Gaddafi. The general strategy boils down to *Look! Gaddafi's son is re-educating terrorists*. Whatever the hell that means. This is a bad idea, a Hail Mary into the North African end zone, but it's the only one I've got at the moment.

When he's back stateside, Labash gives me a call. "It was spooky as shit," he says. "We were surrounded by security the whole time. We were pretty sure they bugged our hotel rooms. There were pictures of Gaddafi everywhere. As ubiquitous as Stop signs."

Ten days before Christmas, I open the *Weekly Standard* at Commissary. The first line of Labash's article seems to be a shout-out to me: "Surely there are worse PR gigs than flacking for the Libyan government, but I can't think of many." It gets worse from there. Labash calls Muammar Gaddafi "a pock-marked F. Murray Abraham-with-a-jheri-curl doppelgänger who looked like he'd swallowed a fistful of Clozapine" and mentions that Gaddafi once called Condoleezza Rice "my little black African woman." Labash writes 750 words. I win maybe ten of them for my client.

A room with black walls. I'm tied to a chair. I can't move my extremities, and I'm very thirsty. A bright yellow light burns down into my eyes. A shadowy form appears behind the light and gradually becomes a man. The Doctor brings his face close to mine. I can smell his cigarette breath. The cologne he's bathed in.

"You think you can steal from kings?" he asks. He grabs my hair and yanks back my head, exposing my throat. He pushes a nickel-plated Beretta against my temple.

Then I hear Doc Brown's voice echo through the room, "The Libyans!"

I wake up on my couch clutching my Opus plush toy. The nightmare stays with me all day. And I have it again the next night. I wonder if I'm going to start seeing faces in my soup or, more likely, my mega mimosas at Commissary. I've been drinking plenty of them.

After a borderline-psychotic stretch of work, most people would head for Cancún. Maybe a relaxing week in Hawaii. I fly to Sarajevo.

The first thing I notice in Sarajevo are the bombed-out, shot-up buildings. I feel like I'm heading into an active war zone. A few hours later, while I'm riding a rumbling bus coughing its way down poorly paved streets, a Bosnian Muslim guide tells me that the Bosnians left their city this way intentionally. To let the world know what happened. And what's still possible. The bus is carrying a U.S. congressional staff delegation, here to tour recent history. BLJ's Turkish client has sponsored the visit to highlight the genocide of Turkic Muslims by the Bosnian Serb Army of Republika Srpska (VRS) during the Yugoslav Wars between 1991 and 2001. An "awareness campaign," we call it in PR, to open American eyes.

For once, I'm on the side of the good guys. This good guy happens to be writing a pretty big check, but still.

That night I eat dolma and flatbread at a restaurant with

a view of the mountains surrounding Sarajevo. The sun sets through the V of a wide canyon, casting the cityscape in burning orange.

"You see the geography?" my Bosnian guide asks. "The way the hills hug the city?"

"It's really beautiful," I say.

"No," he says flatly. "It just makes genocide easier. All the VRS had to do was line the canyons with tanks and artillery and then shell the civilians into submission."

Each site we visit in Sarajevo follows this disturbing pattern: whenever I point out a beautiful square or a striking church, a Bosniak tells me it played some role in the genocide. The bus arrives at a soccer pitch in the town of Srebrenica. I walk out onto the grass, smelling the wet earth. Our guide says the VRS used this field as a holding pen for mass executions. "This place was a river of blood," he says.

Standing on the pitch, I can still imagine people screaming. I'm confronted with the gritty reality of totalitarian power. People are murdered. Thrown into mass graves. And the truth is, nobody pulls the trigger a few million times without help. Operators like me oil the machines that prop up authoritarian power all over the world. I help those machines function by laundering the sins of dictators through the press. I attack their enemies. Provide backdoor access to Washington.

I've done it for Gaddafi, and BLJ is doing it right now for a host of other foreign baddies. Peter Brown's creed "Everyone deserves representation" has been pushed to the extreme. In addition to the Gaddafis, BLJ's clients have included Syrian president Bashar al-Assad; Ali Bongo, president of Gabon, who paid the firm in briefcases full of cash; and the Chinese Communist Party–funded China–United States Exchange Foundation. Though, in one pitch meeting, we did turn down the government of Sri Lanka after one of its senior officials referred to ethnic Tamils as parasites and advocated for their extinction.

I'm only one cog in the machine that powers this system. But I'd be lying to myself if I didn't admit that I'm a very useful cog. In DC, penned up in a posh conference room, I can ignore these pesky moral concerns. Here in Bosnia, where you can feel the blood in the ground, it's not so easy.

This is what the business end of my business looks like.

How long will it be before people tour sites like this soccer stadium, but in Libya or Syria? I'm not sure I can keep doing this. Part of me craves the risk and the adrenaline rush I get from this work. The other part of me is screaming to get out.

But back in DC, the next time Peter Brown calls, I pick up the phone. He gives orders. I'm the blunt instrument who carries them out. If nothing changes, nothing changes, right?

Nothing changes.

Then I meet Lindsay on a blind date.

I ask Lindsay to meet me at Logan Tavern. It's a few doors down from Commissary, ensuring I won't violate my perimeter, in case this goes sideways. I'm sitting at the bar next to a fast-talking brunette who strikes me as being much, much smarter than me. Her hair is perfectly straight, cut tight above her shoulders, not one strand out of place.

Lindsay tells me she debated in high school. In Omaha, Nebraska. And she loves *Star Wars*. It's midsummer 2010, a few weeks after my thirty-first birthday. Lindsay is twenty-eight. Like me, she's spent nearly a decade in DC, though she chose the good-guy route. Currently, she is the communications director for congressman Steve Israel.

"So, you were on the debate team, too?" she asks.

"I was. I was nearly a state champion, but I walked out of the room to prove a point."

"Well, that sounds like a dumb move. Why didn't you take the win?"

We debate about debate, and I start planning our second date in my head. I don't tell her much about what I do for a living. Like everyone else in DC, I assume Lindsay is a dyed-in-the-wool liberal who wouldn't take kindly to my client list. When the bill comes, I grab it, and Lindsay asks me if I'm a lobbyist. She confesses that she did her research before our date and knows that I have, indeed, once been registered as a lobbyist.

"If you still are, we have to split brunch," she says. "I work on the Hill. It's against the rules."

"Oh, I'm not," I assure her, which is technically true.

I don't mention that I'm registered as an agent representing a murderers' row of foreign dictators, a fact that would probably get her into much more trouble.

"Can I ask you something?" I say as I hail Lindsay a cab. I wonder if she's noticed my limp, the way I favor my left leg.

"I'm not going to kiss you on a first date."

"It's something else entirely."

"What's up?"

"How do you feel about skydiving?"

Lindsay is at 15,000 feet harnessed to a guy called Batman. Thirty minutes ago, she very reluctantly signed a twenty-page waiver stating that she will not sue Batman's employer in the event of her untimely death. A jumpmaster throws open the door of the Cessna. People start jumping out. Each time, I feel the plane jostle. Get lighter.

"Okay, this is really happening," Lindsay shouts.

"Do you want to jump first? Or me?" I yell above the rush of wind.

"I've got this. I'll go."

"Let's do it," Batman says. And he and Lindsay jump out into the blue.

I follow them out into the void. The wind hits my ears, and then I'm flying, flying, above a stretch of fields in New Paltz, New York. I've jumped out of dozens of airplanes, and I've never felt any fear. Not because I think I'm Tom Cruise. Rather, every time, part of me hopes the chute won't open. My worst impulses will be realized, and I won't be the one who made the decision. It'll be quick. It won't hurt. And the view will be amazing right up until the end.

But this time, I see Lindsay and Batman free-falling a

few hundred feet below, and suddenly, I'm terrified. It's much scarier to jump out of a plane when you have someone you want to see again back on the ground. Someone you want to live for.

My chute whooshes open, and I glide earthward. I land within fifteen feet of Lindsay, on a patch of muddy grass near the airport runway. Batman unhooks her harness. She wobbles into my arms, shaking with adrenaline, and kisses me.

"Let's do it again," she says.

For months, I hold Lindsay off from seeing my apartment. When she walks in for the first time, she clocks the blank walls, the unframed *Bloom County* posters, the couches draped in sheets to hide the fact that I found them on the sidewalk, the beat-up table, and the empty spaces. The entire place is coated with concrete dust, courtesy of the workers sandblasting bricks outside.

"When did you move in?"

"Five years ago."

"Oh, okay," she says.

Like a press secretary at a tough briefing, I hope for no further questions. Instead of an interrogation, Lindsay decides we'll go furniture shopping.

In the meantime, we stick to her place in Columbia Heights, a neighborhood a mile north of mine. When Lindsay moves to New York to run Steve Israel's reelection campaign, we stay at a series of alliterative hotels: the Smithtown

Sheraton, the Huntington Hilton, the Melville Marriott. Steve Israel wins his race by a wide margin in a year when many Democrats are sent packing. He gets appointed chairman of the Democratic Congressional Campaign Committee, which makes him one of the highest-ranking members of the House of Representatives. Lindsay helped guide his path to leadership.

I like everything about Lindsay. I like that she can hold her own on the Hill and then come home to watch *The Empire Strikes Back* with me. I like that when we plan our first vacation together, we choose a destination where we can hang out on a secluded beach with monkeys.

I like Lindsay so much that I hide things about myself. For example, I often can't get out of bed in the morning. I don't tell Lindsay I now have thirty thousand dollars in credit card debt, or that I have to keep working for dictators because I need the money. That I'm too scared to change, that I'm not normal. I don't tell Lindsay any of this because I'm definitely in love with her, and I definitely don't want her to leave me.

I'm sitting next to an open window in my apartment at Logan Circle, smoking a bowl, when Peter Brown calls.

"I'm just leaving a meeting with the number one man in Doha," he says.

I assume Brown is referring to Hamad bin Khalifa Al Thani, the emir of Qatar. When working for Brown, assumptions are necessary. Peter isn't one to elaborate on his associates or his own whereabouts. I usually have to guess his position on the globe by the sonic frequency of the ringing tone when I call his cell. This meeting with "the number one man" could have taken place in Doha. Or Switzerland. Or the emir's estate in London. But that's beside the point. If Brown's calling me, the emir needs something. And Brown needs a blunt instrument to make it happen.

"Phil, were you aware that Congress passed a resolution supporting the American bid to host the World Cup?"

"I was not," I say. "Who gives a shit about House resolutions? They don't actually do anything."

"Our client is very angry."

"Perhaps they should call a lobbyist."

"Indeed. I want you to run the no-fingerprints campaign. Kneecap the American bid."

"Who's spearheading the U.S. bid?" I ask.

"Bill Clinton."

"Wasn't aware he was a soccer fan."

Brown ignores the joke. "I need you to have one of your men in Washington get a resolution introduced into the U.S. Congress opposing their own bid to host the games," he tells me in a tone you'd use to ask someone to pass the salt.

"That's impossible. You may as well ask me to get a resolution passed requiring children to burn the American flag in school."

"I said it. You make it true."

The line goes dead. I walk to the Fox and Hounds, a bar known for serving a glass of booze with a little mixer on the side. I order a vodka soda and find a table outside to think. It's a bright fall day, just after three in the afternoon. Seventeenth Street is crowded with schoolkids liberated from the classroom; they are pushing one another on the sidewalk. As I sip my drink, pondering the impossibility of this assignment, a pack of kids walks by my table. Several of them are morbidly obese. I remember a commercial I saw that morning in which Michelle Obama implored America's youth to "get moving."

I run inside and ask the bartender for a stack of napkins and a pen.

CHAPTER 5

Thanks, Michelle

"Fat kids! The answer is fat kids!"

"What are you talking about?"

I've called my manager at BLJ from the Fox and Hounds patio. I'm clutching a stack of cocktail napkins covered in scribbling. In the last twenty minutes, I've written a draft of a congressional resolution.

I jump up from the table, smacking it with my knees and rattling the empty glasses. "Twenty percent of children in the United States are considered overweight or obese," I nearly shout into the phone, holding the napkins up to the light coming from the bar. "The United States' failure to fully fund K-through-twelve physical education programs while instead lobbying to host international sports events is harmful to the welfare of our nation's children. Until K-through-twelve physical education is fully funded, no taxpayer money should be spent in the pursuit of hosting international sports events, including the Olympics or the World Cup."

I got the idea from First Lady Michelle Obama's Let's Move! campaign's Task Force on Childhood Obesity. I walk my manager through the strategy. Influencing a World Cup bid requires a highly targeted attack. Only twenty-two members of the FIFA Executive Committee vote on the final decision. Normally, twenty-four officials vote, but two committee members have been suspended for taking bribes. Too bad. They would likely have been solid Qatar supporters.

Delegations present bids in Zurich the day before the vote. Then the committee meets for a few precious hours before announcing two winners. During that tiny window in Zurich, we need to convince the voters that the American government is hesitant to fund a World Cup bid. Right now, Qatar is hopelessly outgunned by Bill Clinton's charm offensive. But the United States is a democracy; Qatar is not. My objective isn't to put my finger on the Qatari side of the scale, but to take weight off the American side. Ironically, I want to do this by loading fat kids onto it.

"It could throw sand in their gears," my manager says. "But we need to get the resolution introduced, like, yesterday."

He's right. The vote is in two weeks. We are running out of time.

"How much money do I have to play with here?" I ask.

"Can you make ten thousand work?"

"I can try."

When you need quick access to Congress, you need a lobbyist. When you need to charm a lobbyist, you take them to the Palm. I arrive at the steakhouse a half hour early. A maître d' who reminds me of the concierge at the Bellagio guides me past walls decorated with cartoon portraits of DC luminaries. Above my table, a cartoon Tom Brokaw stares down at me. I doubt he approves of today's journalistic ethics. I fidget under Brokaw's gaze, craving a cigarette, but Morton's is the only steakhouse in DC where you can still smoke.

The lobbyist arrives, an aging guy in a black suit. We connected through a friend who specializes in third-party outreach and whom I'll call Joe. Actually, his real name is Joe, so let's call him Frank. Lobbyists sell access to politicians; Frank sells access to lobbyists. I'm sure someone farther down the food chain sells access to Frank.

The lobbyist orders a bowl of bone marrow soup and a rib eye. "Should we get a bottle of the Super Tuscan?" he asks, testing the waters of my budget with the wine list.

"Order two," I say.

We're a bottle and a half deep before I make my ask. "I need a resolution introduced about physical education funding," I say.

"Resolutions aren't too tough. Has to be someone aligned with the message. Usually, a bit of back-and-forth on the language."

"Here's the thing. We need it done fast."

The lobbyist studies my face and narrows his eyes, perhaps detecting the scent of duplicity. Or he's raising his price in his head. "What's the rush?" he asks.

"Ink. We need to galvanize the press."

"Who's your client?"

"The Healthy Kids Coalition," I say. "A children's advocacy organization fighting childhood obesity. It's Michelle Obama's big cause."

Technically, I'm not lying. But only technically. The Healthy Kids Coalition doesn't exist. It's a dormant astroturf organization created by some company years ago to advance a completely unrelated legislative agenda. In reality, it is just a website with a tax filing in Delaware. Astroturf organizations are shell nonprofits used to create the illusion of grassroots support for a cause. PR pros use them as shields for our clients. I'm borrowing the Healthy Kids Coalition for a week.

"So, who are you thinking about?" I ask.

"Kilpatrick might do it."

I know all about Detroit representative Carolyn Cheeks Kilpatrick and her family. My parents live just outside Detroit, and Kilpatrick's son, Kwame, was the city's mayor until he was convicted of obstruction of justice. Kwame charged a city-issued credit card $210,000 for massages at spas and for wines as pricey as the one the lobbyist and I are drinking tonight. In 2003, he was connected to the unsolved murder of a stripper who allegedly danced at his mansion, a story that has since become Detroit urban legend. His mother, Representative Kilpatrick, has just lost her primary. She's a lame duck in a lame-duck session. Double lame duck. You can get them to do anything.

"Perfect," I say.

"Me taking this to Kilpatrick costs twenty-five."

"Listen," I say. "I'm working on behalf of these kids. Their mothers don't have a lot of money. All they have is ten K."

There are greater sins than deceiving a lobbyist. Although, this particular sin may cause a sitting congresswoman to unknowingly introduce legislation on behalf of a foreign government.

"The rate is twenty-five."

I take a check for ten thousand dollars out of my pocket and slide it across the linen tablecloth. The lobbyist stares at it while chewing a bite of steak. Ten thousand birds in the hand are better than twenty-five thousand in the bush. He swallows his meat and pockets the check.

I can't attest to whether money changed hands between Kilpatrick and the lobbyist, but a few days later, a draft of the resolution is circulating in the U.S. House of Representatives. My idea has gone from a cocktail napkin to Congress in less than a month.

I don't have time to wait for the resolution to get introduced, so I offer *Politico*'s Ben Smith a leaked copy; I know he's a soccer fan. This is well before Ben Smith became the first editor in chief of *BuzzFeed News* and broke stories

a few other legal *t*'s and *i*'s were not crossed and
knew this because my client knew this; he had the
s needed to obtain this information. All I needed
e appropriate messenger.

ashington is littered with nonprofit organizations
led with the ideal of changing the world for the better.
ideals don't keep the lights on. Money does. My client
ew this. A significant private donation yielded a press
lease from a legitimate nonprofit and a letter of inquiry
to the Department of Justice. Suddenly, my client's enemy
was less concerned with my client and more concerned with
their own growing legal bills.

One afternoon over cocktails, I told Peter Brown this
story.

"You're an arsonist," he pronounced. "Let me see the picture of you and the First Lady of Mexico."

I passed my phone to Brown and took another drink of
wine.

"What are you telling her to make her laugh?" he asked.

"Don't remember," I said. "Sorry."

"I have a guess or two."

Clients ask for hit pieces all the time. Walmart likes to
see negative articles about Amazon. So, in 2018, it hired PR
pros to create the Free and Fair Markets Initiative (FFMI),
which described itself as a "nonprofit watchdog committed
to scrutinizing Amazon's harmful practices and promoting
a fair, modern marketplace that works for all Americans."
Don't be shocked: FFMI was another astroturf organization.

for the *New York Times*

reporter always eager to lan

"How would you like an

opposes the U.S. bid to host the

"That's a weird story," he says.

"Weird enough to interest you?"

"Sure."

"One thing. Would you mind printing n

tion in your article? I think it's important for

Smith confirms with Kilpatrick's office t

is the real thing. His piece is published forty-e

before the vote in Zurich. The headline reads, "Wo

vs. Gym Class?" Smith prints the entire resolution. "

fore, in order to help realize the goals of First Lady Miche

Obama's vision for reducing childhood obesity the US wil

place a higher priority on physical education programs in

public schools," I read. I remember writing those words while

ordering my second vodka soda at the Fox and Hounds. Now

everyone reading *Politico* thinks the words came from the

mouth of a congresswoman and that Michelle Obama is on

our side.

I've got a solid hit piece in my black-ops campaign

against the United States' World Cup bid. PR pros invest a

great deal of time and effort to bring hit pieces to fruition.

Most often, clients want to see a hit piece on their primary

competitor. Early on in my time working for Peter Brown, I

needed to hit one of my clients' political enemies. My adver-

sary did not exactly follow the letter of the law. Their tax

PR pros get well paid for creating these shell nonprofits—in this case, $250,000. FFMI put out a stream of content hitting Amazon: Labor issues. Controversial items being sold on Amazon. Scandals in the C-Suite. All highlighted in tweets, press releases, and media statements by the FFMI.

Normally, this would have been a win. There's a catch. Often, clients don't understand what they are getting themselves into when they commission hit pieces. You must look at every story you pitch as a potential Pandora's box. You won't find out exactly what's inside until you open it. These are the risks when you play this game. Unintended consequences are to be expected. When a good journalist begins to look at the industry writ large, controversies about the client can come into play. Sometimes, the investigation spirals out of control. The hit piece against a competitor can turn on the client. If that happens, you have lost control of the narrative. "Be careful he who hunts monsters, lest ye become a monster yourself." Or whatever Nietzsche said. If you play with fire, there is a better-than-even chance you will get burned.

Sometimes, the ensuing headline can hit the wrong target—which is exactly what happened when Walmart tried to burn Amazon. The *Wall Street Journal*'s headline read, "A 'Grass Roots' Campaign to Take Down Amazon Is Funded by Amazon's Biggest Rivals." The subhead was worse: "Walmart, Oracle, and Mall Owner Simon Property Group Are Secret Funders Behind a Nonprofit that Has Been Highly Critical of the E-Commerce Giant." The reporter had done his job and sniffed out the astroturf organization, including the pesky little detail that one of the "grassroots advocates" had been dead for months. Walmart got hit by its own hit piece, and so did its allies.

Luckily, my hit piece against the United States' World Cup bid is a clean shot, and the Healthy Kids Coalition provides adequate cover. The astroturf nonprofit issues a press release lauding Kilpatrick's vital work on behalf of young arteries. The release appears to come from childhood obesity experts instead of, say, the Qatari royal family.

My manager at BLJ prints dozens of copies of the article and flies to Zurich. The Qatari delegation brings the article to their final meetings with FIFA. They tell the voters that, in America, funding for the World Cup has become a political football. In Qatar, the emir decides how money gets spent.

I watch the announcement broadcast alone on a dirty couch in my apartment on Logan Circle. FIFA president Sepp Blatter announces the 2018 winner first: Russia.

It's a bit of a shock and dashes my hopes for the Qataris. If FIFA awarded a bid to Russia, surely the next one will be for the United States. The balance of power, so to speak.

Then Blatter opens the second envelope. When the name "Qatar" appears, I'm as shocked as the rest of the world. A camera pans over the celebrating Qataris, and I spot Bill Clinton in the shot, whispering something in his aide's ear. Later, Peter Brown tells me that Clinton threw a tchotchke through a mirror in his hotel room that evening.

I don't blame him. The 2010 World Cup vote will be largely regarded as the most corrupt in the history of soccer. The Department of Justice will go on to conduct a multiyear investigation and indict three FIFA officials who received cash to vote for Qatar.

A few days after the announcement, I get a call from one of BLJ's vice presidents. "Did you hear about the seven-figure win bonus in the contract?" she asks.

"I had not. Are we all getting raises?"

"Ha. When Peter tried to collect, the Qataris told him, 'You should read your contracts.' When the Qataris sent back the contract, they had redlined the bonus. Nobody checked."

BLJ has just helped Qatar secure a World Cup bid for the firm's monthly retainer of $80,000. Eventually, Qatar will spend $220 billion on the games. Our fee was a hell of a bargain, if you ask me.

It doesn't matter what happens on the soccer pitch in 2022; Qatar has already won the World Cup. This is about so much more than sports. The Qatar monarchy has been legitimatized in the eyes of the world. As many as 1.5 billion people will watch the 2022 World Cup final. When, in 2023, Qatar's sovereign wealth fund buys a stake in the ownership group of the NBA's Washington Wizards and the NHL's Capitals, nobody bats an eye. Sportswashing works.

The Syrian embassy is a redbrick colonial-style building with white trim. It's not in the Watergate. So that's an upgrade. I fold three hundred dollars into a reporter's passport and hand it to the visa officer. I've gotten to know this officer quite well over the last few months. He's a soccer fanatic.

"What do you think of Doha hosting the World Cup?" I ask him.

"We are proud our region will host the games," he says and hands me back the passport with a visa installed and the hundred-dollar bills gone.

BLJ is sending *Vogue* journalist Joan Juliet Buck to Damascus. The magazine is going to feature our client Asma al-Assad in its March 2011 issue, thanks to Peter Brown calling up his old friend Anna Wintour. The theme of the issue is "Power." We're using the wife of Syrian president (read: dictator) Bashar al-Assad to try to strengthen the relationship between the United States and Syria. It's an American tactic: the First Lady is always more popular than the president, and she makes her husband look good by association.

The *Vogue* story runs under the title "A Rose in the Desert." When I pick up a copy of the glossy magazine, I'm gobsmacked by the first line of the piece: "Asma al-Assad is glamorous, young, and very chic—the freshest and most magnetic of first ladies," the writer gushes. In the first few paragraphs alone, the piece describes Mrs. al-Assad as "breezy" and "fun" and calls Syria "a secular country where women earn as much as men and the Muslim veil is forbidden in universities, a place without bombings, unrest, or kidnappings, but its shadow zones are deep and dark."

The piece reads like the reporter spent a few days with Gwyneth Paltrow: "Asma al-Assad empties a box of fondue mix into a saucepan for lunch," Buck writes. "The household is run on wildly democratic principles. 'We all vote on what we want, and where,' she [Asma] says." (For example, her children voted to make the chandelier over the dining table out of cut-up comic books.) It's rare that you send a journalist on a propaganda tour and they actually print the propaganda. But you won't find any complaints from the flaks who set it all up.

The *Vogue* writer says Mrs. al-Assad likely has a "killer IQ." Poor choice of words when describing a dictator's wife. The article is chock-full of questionable journalistic choices. It quotes Bashar al-Assad himself saying he became an eye surgeon because there is "very little blood." *Vogue* publishes photos of Assad playing with his children: he is dressed like an American president in jeans and a gray fleece.

A few days after the *Vogue* issue hits magazine stands, the Arab Spring revolution erupts in Syria. Thousands of protesters soon fill the streets of Damascus, calling for Assad's head. When his troops beat them bloody, the world reacts live on Twitter. Later, *Vogue* tries to scrub any record of the article's existence from the internet, and Anna Wintour has to defend herself in the pages of the *New York Times*.

In Libya, the Arab Spring escalates to civil war after Gaddafi's army opens fire on protesters in Benghazi, killing hundreds. I think back to Srebrenica, to standing on the blood-soaked soccer pitch. That day, I wondered how long it would be before similar scenes played out in Libya and Syria. It took less than a year. The nature of these conflicts was different; the results were the same. Blood on the soccer pitch. Blood in the desert. It's still blood.

Once again, I'm faced with the business end of my business.

Unfazed, BLJ will go on to advise the Assad regime on how to spin the Arab Spring. Brown wants me to work on the Assad account, but after I find out that the Syrian government is shooting its own people, I refuse to sign the FARA form. In an internal document leaked by Julian Assange and WikiLeaks, BLJ later advises Assad, "If hard power is necessary to quell rebellion, soft power is needed to reassure the Syrian people and outside audiences that reform is proceeding apace, legitimate grievances are being addressed and taken seriously, and that Syria's actions are ultimately aimed at creating an environment in which change and progress can take place." BLJ wants to spearhead media efforts to "create a reform 'echo-chamber' by developing media coverage outside of Syria that points to the President's difficult task of wanting reform, but conducted in a non-chaotic, rational way." All this during a revolution that is quickly becoming a civil war.

Peter Brown wants to meet me at the bar at the Mandarin Oriental. In the middle of a workday. A typical request coming from me. A strange one coming from Peter. On my way to the bar, I see a junior BLJ staffer. Brian is a few years younger than me, hired about a year after I came aboard. We pass in the marble hallway. I catch his eye.

"Peter's firing me, isn't he?" I ask.

"Absolutely," Brian says.

We shake hands, and Brian heads for the exit. I walk through the gilded doors of the bar to face the music. Peter isn't at the bar. It's empty. A waiter comes up to me and asks if I'd like a drink.

"Yes, I think I would," I say. "I'll take a double Pappy Van Winkle. On the rocks."

I sip my two-hundred-dollar glass of bourbon and stare at the ice cubes bobbing in the amber liquor. Peter arrives ten minutes later. He waves the waiter away. I wait for him to speak.

"The Arab Spring has been bad for our business model," he says.

"I agree."

"And as you know, I haven't been happy with your performance for some time."

"I didn't know that, Peter," I say. "I didn't know that at all."

"So, you're out."

Peter Brown gave me a new life the day we met at the Four Seasons. Now he's taking that life away at the Mandarin Oriental. He knows I won't make a scene here.

While Brown explains that he wants me to stay on for two weeks to smooth out the transition, I am thinking, *This man describes me to clients as a hit man. A guy who can punch hard in the media.* I want to turn to him and say, "For years, you've called me an arsonist. What do you think I'm about to do?"

I hold my tongue. Even now, even as he's casting me out into the cold, I'm still in awe of Peter Brown.

I cab it home and head down to the computer lab in the basement of my apartment building. I enter the password to my BLJ email account. I need to get it all before they lock me out. I start forwarding documents to my personal email account. I'm looking for anything with an attachment. Anything from Peter. Thirty minutes later, I've forwarded 1,500 communications that Peter would never want to see the light of day.

Then I start printing. Invoices paid by the Gaddafis, Assad, Gabon. The printer hums and clicks. Soon, I've got a stack fifty pages thick. I slip it into a manila envelope and lick the seal.

I ask Lindsay to meet me at Commissary the next day for lunch. I arrive an hour early and start drinking. By the time she arrives, I'm in a gray area between tipsy and buzzed.

Lindsay and I have been seeing a lot of each other. We've talked about my moving into her place when her roommate moves out. Lindsay looks happy to see me. Then she notices the graveyard of glasses.

"You okay?" she asks.

"I'm going to do something," I say.

"Oh . . . Phil."

"Burn a few bridges."

"You're going to inform on BLJ?"

"To every reporter who'll take my call. At the biggest papers I can."

"I'm not going to tell you how to run your life," Lindsay says. "But it's generally a good rule to avoid leaving a trail of destruction in your wake."

"Peter is doing something wrong. I mean look at the Middle East right now. Blood on the streets. Assad is shooting civilians."

"Didn't you rep Assad as of, like, last Tuesday?"

"It's the right thing to do to hold Peter accountable."

"That's why you're doing this? Accountability?"

"Bingo."

"You want to know what I think?"

"By all means," I say.

"I think you're pissed at Peter. I think you're doing this out of spite."

"It's the right thing to do," I repeat.

"Phil, this could hurt your future. Move on. Let go."

Lindsay is right, of course. About everything. Here's the thing about good advice: sometimes, you just can't take it. I start dialing reporters later that afternoon.

The first reporter I meet with has rules. Rule number one: If there is alcohol on the table, the conversation is off the record. Better than fine by me. We've met at the Bottom Line, a dive bar where I used to pick up an occasional shift while at Georgetown. There is most certainly alcohol on the table.

"Gaddafi and Assad's PR guy, the former manager of the Beatles, selectively registered their accounts with the Department of Justice," I say. "This is a problem."

"Why are you telling me this?"

"Because he just fired me."

Part of my strategy in dealing with reporters is to express my agenda up front. I'm honest about my conflicts of interest. I often tell reporters, "This is the headline I'd like to read. This is the reason I'm talking to you. This is my motivation. And yes, someone is paying me to say this. But here's the story." Why not be up front about my motives? It gives me immediate credibility. It gets dirty laundry out in the open so they don't find it later. Playing hide the football with someone who investigates people like me for a living is a bad idea. And what comes after "But here's the story" is usually newsworthy. I'm never trying to sell toothpaste or bananas.

I tell the reporter how much Gaddafi paid BLJ. I tell them about babysitting the Doctor in Las Vegas. And I tell them that we didn't register any of this with the Department of Justice. I go through, in detail, each of the questionable things I have been asked to do while working at Brown Lloyd James. The payments in cash. The mysterious emails. The "nontraditional business practices." Peter Brown is an eccentric man, one who firmly believes there are two sets of rules: one for those with money and another for the rest of the world. Neither set of rules really applies to him.

"Are you sure you want to do this?" the reporter asks. "These are scary people."

"The real question is, Do you want the story?"

People always ask for my motives. They want to know why. Here's the truth, a truth I have trouble admitting and explaining: I do it for the story. My time with Brown Lloyd James cannot end with the whimper of my making Peter Brown pay for my two-hundred-dollar glass of whiskey. I need it to end with a bomb. It's not that I'm upset about being fired. Rather, it's about *who* fired me. The caliber of the person who fires you matters. Later in life, I will be terminated by a bureaucrat at one of the mega firms. I had so little respect for this person that I thanked him for firing me. But for some reason, being dismissed by a rock-and-roll icon has set something off in me. This story needs a proper ending.

"You didn't answer the question," the reporter says.

"My safety is not my first concern."

"Well, regardless of your motivation, there *is* a story here. BLJ is flouting the law. And they are unlikely to get caught."

I push the manila envelope across the table. "Everything you need is in here."

The article goes live on September 9, 2011. "The public-relations firm Brown Lloyd James posts an extensive client roster on its website, including composer Andrew Lloyd Webber, the charity Autism Speaks, Carnegie Mellon University and the state of Qatar," it begins. "Unacknowledged on its website client list is its work for the regime of Libya's Col. Moammar Gadhafi and the wife of Syrian President Bashar al-Assad." The work BLJ does, the piece reads, "carries a risk to a firm's reputation, especially if a firm's client battles

its citizens, as happened in both Syria and Libya this year."
The reporter got Tony Fratto, a Treasury and White House
spokesman during the Bush administration, to comment on
Peter Brown's business practices. "To me the job of diplomatic relations with foreign governments, even troubled
ones, is the job of the State Department," Fratto says.

Peter liked to call me an arsonist. Now he's got a fire.

The Department of Justice refuses to confirm if Brown
Lloyd James will face sanctions or penalties due to its failure to properly register clients. I hear rumors over the next
weeks that the U.S. government has called BLJ with some
questions. Staffers there are frantically emailing to get all
their records updated for the DOJ. But in the end, Brown
files the appropriate forms, apparently having convinced
the DOJ that there was no intentional evasion of the law.
All crimes are forgiven. And the system will keep turning.
Influence will be purchased. Governments will topple. And
the people living under dictatorships will continue to suffer
and die.

My career as a bagman for dictators is over. But I can't
get out of public relations. I'm still in debt. This is the only
way I know how to make money. Who else will employ me
after what I've done? The Hill won't have me back, but the
PR industry embraces me. And that's what happens when
I walk through the doors of Levick Strategic Communications, the premier crisis communications shop in DC. I tell
the firm's CEO Richard Levick, about my work on the Qatari
World Cup bid. He's impressed.

* * *

On May 13, 2011, while I'm filling out new-hire paperwork
with Levick, NATO aircraft strike Gaddafi's Bab al-Aziziya
compound in Tripoli. Gaddafi responds by taunting NATO. "I
tell the cowardly crusader [NATO] that I live in a place they
cannot reach and where you cannot kill me," he says in an
audio recording played on Libyan state-run TV.

Turns out, he was right. For about three months.

Tripoli falls in August. Gaddafi and Mutassim flee to the
desert city of Sirte. At approximately 8:30 a.m. local time on
October 20, NATO forces intercept a satellite phone call made
by the Brother Leader. At the same time, a Royal Air Force
reconnaissance mission spots an ever-so-subtle seventy-
five-car motorcade blasting through the desert. An American Predator drone circling the skies over Libya, operated
by someone in Las Vegas, fires at the convoy first. It is the
middle of the night in Sin City, where I spent my terrifying
weekend with Mutassim. Moments later, French fighter jets
bomb the convoy. Gaddafi hides in a drainage pipe before
being captured by rebels.

The next day, I follow the news. The networks show a
photo of the Doctor's dead body, shot in the chest and the
neck. I wonder what's become of Ali and the two Muhammads. I have a feeling most of the people on our Las Vegas
trip are now dead. Al Jazeera cuts to footage of Muammar
Gaddafi being beaten by rebels, blood pouring down his face
and clumped in his hair. A pistol is put to his head.

His last words are, "Do you know right from wrong?"

CHAPTER 6

The Government v. the Internet

A call from a *Wall Street Journal* reporter wakes me at 5 a.m.

"Phil, I wanted to give you the chance to comment on a story that's about to go live," he says. "Here's our lead: 'After months of planning, New Zealand police swooped on Megaupload founder Kim Dotcom's home as guests arrived to celebrate his birthday.'"

"Let me get some people awake," I croak.

Dotcom's lawyer, Robert S. Bennett, former counsel to President Bill Clinton, fills me in. Counterterrorism agents have raided the Web baron's 25,000-square-foot Auckland mansion using military helicopters, canine units, and SWAT vehicles in an operation coordinated with the FBI. My client barricaded himself in his panic room, clutching a sawed-off shotgun. He faces extradition to the United States on charges of copyright infringement, racketeering, money laundering, and wire fraud.

When you work in crisis communications, you expect the phone to ring with a crisis. Just not this many of them at once.

Six weeks earlier, on a Monday morning in December, I enter Levick Strategic Communications. Our building sits on the corner of Nineteenth and M Streets NW in Washington, DC. Richard Levick's corner office is lined with bookcases stuffed with legal treatises. That day, I join Levick, who is smoothing the lapels of his three-piece suit, and four executives huddled around the speakerphone. A senior vice president gives me the once-over.

"So, you're Richard's new black-ops guy?"

Before I can respond, the speakerphone connects and a German accent punctures the room. Kim Dotcom's voice throws me—not what I'd expected from an obese hacker. I'd assumed he'd sound like Neo from *The Matrix*, not Christoph Waltz from *Inglourious Basterds*.

"I vant to box this little vorm," Kim Dotcom booms.

"Pleasure to meet you, Mr. Dotcom," Levick says.

"Mr. Dotcom's subsidiary Megaporn has been sued by Perfect Ten, a porn company looking to create a new revenue stream as a copyright troll. He's being forced to pay a large settlement," adds Dotcom's tech lawyer, a fast-talking attorney from San Francisco. "Perfect Ten's CEO is on the older side."

"I vill fight him on television for the exact amount of the settlement," Dotcom says through the speakerphone.

The suits around the table exchange frowns. I immediately like the guy. I've finally met a client whose ideas are crazier than mine. As the junior man on this intake call, I remain mute, watching how Levick handles the situation.

"Sounds a tad . . . splashy," says Levick. "What if we got some third-party allies to say good things about you?"

"Put a good face on the settlement while still maintaining a viable business," a VP in the room interjects.

"I am not a criminal," says Dotcom.

"Paying the settlement is not dispositive of guilt," says Levick.

"I have a legitimate business. *Forbes* vants to put me on the cover. I see a vorld where big content and internet freedom can exist together."

"I see that world, too," Levick says. "And we can help the public see it. Let's hold off talking to reporters until the settlement news cycles through the papers. Is there anything else we should know?"

It's a good question. All PR crises start with an intake call. It's an exercise in extracting as much information as we can from the client and their lawyer. Usually your client, or more often their lawyer who is *always* on an intake call, doesn't tell you the whole truth or neglects to tell you something very important. (Case in point: At the time of this meeting, the FBI is six weeks away from taking down Dotcom, and he's already hired a criminal defense team.) Or they straight-up lie to you, trying to play the PR pro with PR pros. Sometimes, I say to lawyers, "Do you see me getting up in the courtroom and making objections? Tell me the truth and let me talk to the media."

"That's where things stand," says Dotcom's lawyer.

"So, nothing else?" asks Levick.

"I vant to move fast," Dotcom says.

"We will turn around a proposal for you in twenty-four hours," Levick says, shooting his finger in my direction.

Proposals are the responsibility of the most junior agent. Twenty-four hours is actually a large window within which to come up with a crisis strategy. I've been through fire drills where a client had to talk to reporters within thirty minutes.

"Start with the crazy on this proposal. I'll rein you in," Levick tells me after the call, over a glass of bourbon. He keeps the good stuff hidden inside a false globe. "I love the way your brain works."

"I can do that."

"Stop by HR on your way out. Tell them you'll need to look at some . . . blocked sites on the company laptop. I don't think Perfect Ten or Megaporn are whitelisted."

I order takeout from Commissary and browse dozens of articles about my new client. Kim Dotcom is my kind of criminal: a six-foot-seven, three-hundred-pound computer nerd who likes chartering model-laden yachts, driving vintage Cadillacs on golf courses, and playing games with the American entertainment industry. In 2005, he started the file-sharing service Megaupload, through which users could access copyrighted content like Hollywood films free of charge. At its peak, Megaupload claimed to have sixty million users, to generate twice as much Web traffic as Facebook, and to have turbocharged Dotcom's net worth to two hundred million. He sometimes travels with a life-size statue of the alien from *Predator*.

Out of all my clients, Kim Dotcom has the longest rap sheet. The man born Kim Schmitz was first convicted in 1998 for trafficking stolen phone card codes, computer fraud, and data espionage. He milked the arrest for hacker cred, telling the press he was the head of an international cybercrime team called Dope. He bragged that he had breached Citibank's digital vaults and sent twenty million dollars to Greenpeace. A 2001 piece in the German newspaper *Die Welt* says he hacked NASA and the Pentagon, accessing classified military intel on Saddam Hussein. The *Guardian* claims he sabotaged the credit rating of former German chancellor Helmut Kohl. In 2002, he was convicted of manipulating the stock of a Dutch internet company. German authorities extradited him from Thailand. He met them at the Munich airport introducing himself as the "Royal Highness Kimble the First."

Kim parlayed exploits into hacker fame. According to *Wired*, "He promoted his new bad-boy rich hacker genius image through a bizarre Flash movie called *Kimble, Special Agent*, in which his cartoon alter-ego drives a 'Megacar' and then a 'Megaboat' before breaking into Bill Gates's compound and riddling the wall behind Gates with a machine gun (spelling out 'Linux' with bullet holes)."

Peter Brown taught me that "anything is possible with the right amount of money." Dotcom has exponentially more money than Peter Brown, and his fortune has allowed him to stay one step ahead of the law since the Clinton administration. We're now well into the Obama administration. Dotcom had successfully skirted the law for three presidents while enjoying wine, women, and song. And he found the time to become the number one–ranked player in the world in *Call of Duty: Modern Warfare 3*. "Don't hate me because I beat you," goes his gamer motto. "Respect me because I can teach you."

A 2001 article in the *Telegraph* calls Dotcom "a PR man's nightmare and a journalist's dream." Conventional PR wisdom says the public should hate him. Not so. He's mostly beloved, even by people who should *really* hate him like Kanye West and Apple's Steve Wozniak, who had money taken out of their pockets by Megaupload. Of course, Dotcom is reviled by the entertainment companies and their lobbyists, like the Motion Picture Association of America, and they have *really* good reasons to detest him. The MPAA estimates that online piracy costs the U.S. film industry around $29.2 billion per year. (Typical of the MPAA, this figure seems like a bit of hyperbole.) But millions of fans on the internet can't get enough of this obese geek who lives like Richie Rich while gleefully flipping the bird to the powers that be.

I, too, am smitten. Dotcom is a PR genius. He breaks every rule of public relations and gets away with it.

Rule 1. Don't believe the lie that "any press is good press."

"There is no such thing as bad press" is the most flawed statement in public relations. Just ask Gaddafi. Except if you are Kim Dotcom. There is no way for a journalist to write about this cartoon character that he won't find flattering. Dotcom lets it all hang out and flips bad stories into irreverent jokes on his Twitter account.

Rule 2. Don't repeat the negative.

Tell me the first Richard Nixon quote that pops into your head. "I am not a crook," right? You remember the line even if you weren't born yet when Nixon said it. Everyone remembers the line. Those five words are perhaps the single greatest PR blunder in American history. Nixon repeated the negative, the first thing in media training we teach clients to avoid doing. If someone asks how long you've been beating your wife, you don't say, "I'm not a wife beater." You say, "I'm a good man." Why deny when you can obfuscate?

Dotcom is often asked if Megaupload is legal. He doesn't say, *I run a legitimate business and donate to charity.* He says, *The law is wrong.* Everything that comes out of Kim Dotcom's mouth is worthy of indictment. Because he tells the truth, he's guilty of most crimes except perjury.

Rule 3. Never wrestle with a pig in shit.*

Two things will happen. You'll be covered in shit. And the

---

* A few versions of this quote are attributed to Irish playwright and critic George Bernard Shaw. The classic version is "I learned long pig will like it. Never get down and fight with an opponent who is beneath you. Dotcom wants to challenge a copyright troll to fisticuffs. He'd probably stream it live on Twitter. And people would root for him.

Rule 4. Don't kick someone when they are up.
An old saying in Washington. It's too much work to attack a strong opponent. Know your place. Dotcom kicks whomever he wants: beloved CEOs, the entertainment industry, powerful lobbies like the MPAA. These are people who hire shadow men like me and tell us, "Do your worst." Even Dotcom's ridiculous surname kicks up at authority. Knowing that his line of work would bring him up against lawsuits and investigations, he legally changed it so the header of any case against him essentially reads, "the Government v. the Internet." He's a complete 180 from humorless dictators sequestered in their bloodstained, oil money palaces.

I can't wait to get started.

At the Willard Hotel's Round Robin Bar, DC bartending legend Jim Hewes serves me one of his gorgeous old-fashioneds. Hewes lives by the motto "Never let the truth get in the way of a good story." I'll drink to that.

I haven't been back to the Willard since BLJ threw

---

ago, never to wrestle with a pig. You get dirty, and besides, the pig likes it." I've always liked this version: "Never wrestle with a pig. The pig is better at it; you both end up smelling like shit; and the pig likes the smell."

Gaddafi the "Hooray, Forty Years as a Dictator!" bash. Fifteen minutes later, the rapper Swizz Beatz enters, wearing the type of suit NBA players wear courtside after they've torn their Achilles'.

"You Phil?" he asks.

"Yeah," I say.

"I'm excited for the multitude of opportunities presented by this opportunity to grow my personal brand."

"Uh-huh," I say.

It's been a busy few weeks. Dotcom settled with Perfect 10. Under Levick's advisement, he did not box its aging, balding CEO. It would have been cruel. Funny. But cruel. Dotcom has bigger plans for Megaupload.

"We're going legit," he announced on a recent conference call. "Mainstream. We're going to install someone with music industry credibility as CEO."

Enter Swizz Beatz. I'm handling the media rollout for Beatz's upcoming announcement as Megaupload's CEO. Swizz Beatz and his nine Grammy nominations are the face of a well-crafted narrative. We're using him as a shield from music industry criticism, creating the narrative that Dotcom is entering the lawful fold. Mega, Kim, and Swizz aren't destroying the music industry; they are the well-meaning stewards of its future. Dotcom's next move is to partner with a record label and major industry figures to release music through his file-sharing platform.

He's off to a hot start. A few days ago, on December 17, Dotcom released the "Megaupload Song" music video to

YouTube. The video stars Kim Kardashian; musical artists Kanye West, will.i.am, P. Diddy, and Chris Brown; actor Jamie Foxx; boxer Floyd Mayweather Jr.; and tennis champ Serena Williams. After the parade of A-listers, Dotcom appears in it dressed in a black hoodie, sporting a neckbeard, and boasting "Four percent of the internet. . . . It's a hit, it's a hit!"

Once again, Dotcom breaks all the rules of PR. He kicks up at the music labels and literally repeats the (potentially criminal) negative in song: "M-E-G-A! Upload to me today!" Artists who have contracts with major record labels are advertising the very company bending those labels over a barrel. I imagine the horrified faces of the United Talent Agency suits logging on and seeing their biggest clients shilling for a pro-piracy website.

Once again, Dotcom gets away with it. The music video racks up millions of views on YouTube. The press covers it as a fun oddity. And the song is an earworm, as if an AI program mixed a commercial jingle with a song by the Black Eyed Peas. Yesterday, I caught Lindsay singing it while she cooked breakfast. "Meeegggaaaa," she hummed. "Me-ga-upload. Send me a file."

"This launch is going to be massive," Swizz Beatz tells me at the Round Robin.

"Don't talk to Page Six," I tell him. "They're sniffing. We'll break the news soon. Thinking of the *Wall Street Journal*. Only right for a CEO."

"I like the sound of that."

I leave the Willard and head to Rumors, a sticky-floored

bar with a patio near Levick's office. I work late, emailing with a tech reporter named Ernesto who writes for *Torrent-Freak* and with a *Forbes* writer who wants to put Dotcom on the magazine's February cover. If all goes according to plan, I'll be on a plane to New Zealand in a few weeks.

All does not go according to plan.

Now, a few days later, I get the call that Kim Dotcom has been arrested. When Dotcom hired Levick, I suspected he didn't need us to deal with just a copyright troll. His lawyers didn't give us the straight dope. Dotcom knew the FBI was trying to take him down. Now that day has come. The day of his arrest, the press runs photos of Dotcom brandishing a shotgun in front of a black Mercedes with a vanity license plate reading, "GUILTY." The music newsletter *Complex* declares it possibly the first case of confession via license plate.

I doubt antics will save him this time. Dotcom threatens multibillion-dollar entertainment companies with deep connections to the White House. Chris Dodd, the chairman and chief lobbyist for the MPAA, was a senator from Connecticut when President Obama was a senator from Illinois. Vice President Joe Biden has called Dodd one of his best friends. Dotcom's lawyer will claim that White House logs show Obama and Dodd meeting in the Oval Office on December 9, just a month before Dotcom's takedown.

Then, around the time of the raid, Dodd went on Fox

News. "Those who count on, quote, Hollywood for support need to understand that this industry is watching very carefully who's going to stand up for them when their job is at stake," he said. "Don't ask me to write a check for you when you think your job is at risk, and then don't pay any attention to me when my job is at stake."

Is it too far into the weeds of conspiracy to think Dodd threatened to yank financial support for the Democrats unless Obama sanctioned the raid? I call Preston to run my theory by him.

"Communist Hollywood and leftist politicians coordinating to destroy an armed sovereign citizen? I don't believe you," he says dryly. "Are you a cognizant freethinking individual? Is this not obvious to you already?"

"What's that noise?" I ask, hearing a pop-pop-pop in the background.

"I'm on a range in Upstate New York. Marine snipers are teaching me to be more effective with long-range rifles. We shoot with silencers, but you can still hear it."

"Sounds accurate."

"We're hitting kill shots at a thousand yards," Preston says. "Hate to tell you, Phil, but you're getting beat at your own game. 'Public relations' is just the genteel name for propaganda. You went up against Hollywood propagandists. They are as rich as Croesus. And they have a bigger army."

"I don't have an army."

"Get one. They've got the FBI. You don't even own a

gun, for some reason that I cannot fathom and will not attempt to."

"I'll work on my army. Right now, I'm scrambling. The press keeps harping on the detail that Kim was arrested holding a sawed-off shotgun. He's like a Bond villain."

"A villain?" Preston says. "He's standing up to the state in an armed fashion. He speaks to me on a deep level. But a sawed-off is a rookie move. It's too fucking loud. And ninety-five percent of people load with bird shot. Nonlethal at twenty-five yards. A longer barrel is better for putting warheads through foreheads."

"For my purposes, it'd be better if Kim didn't brandish a gun at all."

"Don't be ridiculous," he says. "I've got to run. If you're ever in New York and feel like shooting shit at great distances, please let me know."

I manage the crisis through the weeklong news cycle immediately following Dotcom's arrest and garner positive news coverage on his behalf. But there is only so much a PR firm can do when its client is an FBI target. The DOJ instructs us to stop working for Dotcom and freezes his assets. I'm frustrated that my hands are tied. I hate that the justice system does the bidding of media conglomerates.

If I'm being really honest, I'm mostly disappointed that Dotcom and I never had a chance to get started. When I think about the media games we could have played, it's like pining for a long-lost love. I want revenge for my PR white whale. But it's a dumb idea to go after the FBI. And Levick's phone keeps ringing with intake calls from clients in crisis whose assets are not frozen.

Lindsay leads me down a dark linoleum hallway lined with stacks of Plexiglas doors. Scores of desperate-looking cats and tiny kittens look out at us.

"Our guy doesn't do the cute and fuzzy thing," Lindsay says. "He's more gangly and mangy."

"Look at these little guys," I say, stopping in front of two orange tabby brothers licking each other's ears.

"Don't look in their eyes," Lindsay says, yanking my arm. "It's a trap. Besides, they have each other. Our guy doesn't have anyone left. His siblings and mom have been adopted. He's been here for months."

Lindsay has been volunteering at the Washington Animal Rescue League, on a secret mission to find the best cat to adopt. She watches the cats interact with visitors, eavesdrops on the staff discussing the hard-luck cases, and recaps the details to me, cat by cat, at dinner. This is one of the things I love most about Lindsay: her idea of a conspiracy has her embedded in an animal shelter petting stray cats. If I were a double agent, I'd probably wind up working for an Afghan warlord.

Lindsay approaches a cage. A pair of yellow eyes open, staring skeptically. Lindsay unlocks the cage and fishes out a scraggly kitten who can't weigh more than a couple of pounds. He's jet black, all except those eyes.

"I saw him make a kid cry earlier today," Lindsay says,

scooping the kitten onto her shoulder and heading to a side room where we can let him loose. "His name is Humerus, like the bone, but I was thinking we'd call him Darth Vader."

I lean down and reach out. Darth Vader considers me for a moment, then stabs me in the leg with a razor-sharp claw. A trail of blood runs down my shin. A volunteer rushes to bring me a Band-Aid.

"You probably want to meet some other cats," the volunteer says.

"No, this one is an excellent judge of character," I say. "We'll take him."

They put Darth Vader inside a box with holes, and Lindsay and I head home with him.

I moved into Lindsay's place two weeks ago. My *Bloom County* posters have finally found frames. Lindsay leaves me and Darth in the back bedroom. "I'm going to Petco. We need supplies," and she bounds out the door.

I peek through the holes in the box. A yellow eye stares back. I open the box, and Darth Vader beelines it under the couch, which in Lindsay's place is stain-free and not concealed by old sheets.

"I find your lack of faith disturbing," I tell him.

I lie on the bed. The pillowcases smell like Lindsay, clean and fresh and of another scent that makes me feel calm and happy. They smell like home. After fifteen minutes, a dark flash creeps into my peripheral vision. Darth Vader studies me. He approaches, one paw at time. I don't move an eyelash, and he hops onto the bedspread, still keeping his distance. I resist the overwhelming urge to pet.

"You have emotional problems," I tell Darth Vader. "That's cool with me. I do, too."

Lindsay busts through the front door carrying bags of kitty litter, a new litter box filled with toys, food, brushes, and treats. "I spent way too much money, Phil," she shouts, putting things into cabinets. "We now have a Petco credit card."

"Come see," I call out from the bedroom.

Lindsay appears in the doorway and sees Darth Vader lying at my feet. "I think he likes you," she says. "So maybe he won't stab you anymore."

"You're going to be fine. It's going to be fine," Lindsay says.

I sit up on the stretcher, anesthesia already coursing through my veins. But I'm ready. I've been practicing a joke just for this moment. "Next time you see me, they'll be double Ds," I say, grabbing my chest. Lindsay cracks up as orderlies wheel me into the operating room. Then everything goes darker than black.

When I come to, I am hugging my Opus plush toy. Lindsay leans over the hospital bed and snaps a selfie. She tells me the surgery went well; they shaved down the bone spur jamming into the labrum of my hip. This operation will buy me two years until I need a total hip replacement.

"In the waiting room, I read four hundred pages of *Harry*

Potter and the Goblet of Fire," Lindsay says. "I have so much to tell you. And Preston snuck in a bottle of bourbon."

"Bourbon," I repeat, like an alcoholic infant learning his first word.

"Later," she says. "Bourbon later."

"Don't leave," I say. "I don't want to be alone."

Lindsay pulls up old episodes of *Law & Order* on her laptop. She stays with me in the recovery unit all night and falls asleep in her chair with her face pressed into a stack of blankets at the foot of my bed.

A pharmacist hands me a bottle of OxyContin. Forty pills. Then a bottle of Percocet. Ninety pills. Each with two refills. Take one or two every six hours for hip pain. Sure.

I start taking client calls after popping Percocet. I rub the extended-release coating off the Oxys with a wet paper towel and use a spoon to crush the pills into a fine powder that I swallow with water. In this way, the drug rushes into my bloodstream. I grow accustomed to the warm opiate bath running down my spinal cord.

I'm back at the pharmacy the day my bottles run out. I like Percocet. I like Oxy even more. Too much. When my last refill runs dry, I stop cold turkey. I shake. I sweat. I vomit. Four days into my detox, Richard Levick notices me hunched over my desk, my fists clenched into white balls.

"Are you okay?" he asks.

"Just going through withdrawal," I say.

I don't realize it at the time, but I am one of millions of

Americans who were overprescribed opioids by doctors. I get lucky. My parachute opens before I fall headlong into opioid addiction. Now called the first wave of the opioid crisis, the overprescribing began in the late 1990s. Guess what Purdue Pharma debuted in 1996? If you guessed Oxy-Contin, you've won a free Purdue Pharma hat! (*Legal disclaimer: Purdue Pharma LP does not sanction the views of Mr. Philip Elwood, nor is the company liable for any headwear-related giveaways Mr. Elwood promises in his memoir.*)

Karl Marx said religion was the opium of the people. You know what's a lot more like the opium of the people? Opiates. Like every other drug dealer I have ever met, Purdue, and the Sackler family who owned the company, sold a product that people wanted. Turns out the market for legal heroin is huge. But you can't very well take out an advert in the *New York Times* to sell heroin, can you? So, Purdue hired McKinsey and Company and a little-known PR firm called Dezenhall Resources. And Dezenhall Resources helped commandeer the credibility of the American Enterprise Institute, a center-right think tank. Think tanks are research and advisory non-profits, and they litter the streets of downtown DC. There is a think tank for most things you can think about or shoot with a tank. Many think tanks are wonderful resources for scholarship and potential legislation. But they can be corrupted. Some take money for "directed research." In these relationships, there is often a financial stake in the conclusions of the research—a very polite way of saying that a donor is funding the conclusions. Sometimes the donor is a high-net-worth individual with an agenda. Or a corporation with an agenda. Or a foreign nation with an agenda. Nothing is free. Not even for a nonprofit.

For Purdue, the price tag was $800,000. Remember my saying that you can't very well take out an ad in the *New York Times* to sell heroin? Well, not unless that ad is penned by psychiatrist Sally Satel, senior fellow at the American Enterprise Institute and unpaid advisory board member for the Substance Abuse and Mental Health Services Administration. Satel's 2004 *New York Times* piece was titled, "Doctors Behind Bars: Treating Pain Is Now Risky Business." How is this for shifting the narrative? "Pain treatment itself is an area ripe for misinterpretation. Many patients who seek doctors' help have already tried nonsteroid anti-inflammatory drugs, conventional opiates like codeine and even surgery, yet they are still in severe pain from cancer, degenerative arthritis, nerve damage or other conditions," Satel wrote. "Large doses of medicines like hydrocodone (Vicodin), oxycodone (OxyContin), morphine or methadone may be required." Satel actually plugged Oxy by name, and quoted a Purdue shill claiming that one in ten Americans in pain could benefit from a long-term, high-dose treatment with the drug. All I can say is well done.

The overprescribing peaked in 2010. When people ran out of pills, they turned to heroin. Then fentanyl. At least 645,000 people died from opioid overdoses from 1999 through 2021. In the end, McKinsey and Company had to pay over $640 million for its role in the opioid epidemic. Books, news articles, magazine exposés, and even *60 Minutes* have covered the epidemic and the PR machine behind it. I could name more names and shame more people, but I'm a PR guy, so I'd rather look at two press releases: the first one ever written and the one drafted by the Sacklers in 2021.

On Sunday, October 28, 1906, at 2:20 p.m., a West Jersey and Seashore Railroad train derailed and plunged into the Thoroughfare, the creek separating Atlantic City from the mainland, at nearly forty miles per hour. Fifty-three people drowned.

This is where Ivy Lee enters the story.

In the wake of the derailment, Ivy Ledbetter Lee, now regarded as a "father of modern public relations," drafted the first-ever press release. His client was the Pennsylvania Railroad, which owned the West Jersey and Seashore Railroad. The press praised Lee's release for being so transparent and straightforward. So much so that the *New York Times* printed it in its entirety.

Things have changed since then.

On December 9, 2021, the Metropolitan Museum of Art and the Sackler family jointly issued a press release. One might call it the final release of the Sackler era. For fifty years, the Sackler family donated millions to the Metropolitan Museum of Art. But now the Sacklers' evils had come to light, and the time had arrived to announce the removal of the Sackler name from the museum's walls. The Met could have issued a scathing press release, calling the Sacklers drug dealers and murderers. Both accurate statements. Instead, the Sacklers and the Metropolitan Museum of Art apparently negotiated the language of the release. Museum president and CEO Daniel Weiss stated, "The Met has been built by the philanthropy of generations of donors—and the Sacklers have been among our most generous supporters." Weiss called the Sacklers "gracious." Mention of the opiate deaths, or any reason for the museum's stripping the Sackler name from its walls, was conspicuously absent from the text. Compared to the first press release ever drafted, the Met's release shows just how much my industry has changed. Ivy Lee got it right the first time. Now even museums launder the truth and offer their own spin.

The PR industry is a parasite. It lives off its host, the media. But what happens when the parasite becomes bigger than the host? Now, in 2024, the host is evolving. Salaries in some newsrooms are going up. Private equity is buying up media companies left and right. Foreign nations are investing heavily, too. Lines of ethics are blurring. Social media companies are becoming news agencies. Their rosters of investors include some of the most blood-soaked money in the world.

And the PR industry has also begun to publicly invest in new media properties. In 2023, the news media site the Messenger launched, while simultaneously acquiring another news media company called Grid News. Grid News debuted with a great deal of fanfare and some boldface names in reporters, but later it was revealed that one of its principal

backers was the UAE-based International Media Invest-
ments, which will now be a minority investor in the Messenger. The company's majority investors—they brought in fifty
million dollars—were led by the Stagwell Group, a DC-based
holding company controlled by former Burson-Marsteller
CEO Mark Penn. Stagwell in turn owns PR companies, most
notably, SKDK, a DC firm with close ties to the Biden White
House. It's one thing when media corporations are beholden
to sponsors, but quite another when they are beholden to
governments. This adds another layer of conflict. You have
to wonder if the Messenger would ever run critical stories
of the UAE or of SKDK's extensive client list. Their paymas-
ters call their objectivity into question. And SKDK executives do not divest themselves from the firm when they do
government service for the Biden administration, including
prepping Joe Biden for national debates. It's akin to an SEC
regulator giving out stock tips.

This is the battlefield where we play our game. Understanding rivalries between media companies, between PR
firms, between former clients and potential clients. Not to
mention trying to do work for actual clients.

Nearly a year after his arrest, I'm still thinking about Kim
Dotcom. I want to avenge my former client. I'm daydreaming
of ways to do this when I get a phone call from a DC operative who's a friend. He tells me the United States has banned
Americans from gambling in Antigua's online casinos, anni-
hilating $3.4 billion of the tiny Caribbean nation's economy.

Nearly four thousand people (4 percent of the country's population) have lost their jobs, and Prime Minister Baldwin Spencer is up for reelection.

"I told the prime minister my friend Phil solves exotic problems," the operative says.

I see an opportunity to exact revenge on the entertainment industry and to help a hopelessly outgunned underdog. Richard Levick and I are on the next flight to Antigua.

CHAPTER 7

The Internet v. the Government

My pen moves fast, scribbling bullet points onto a yellow legal pad. In the seat next to mine, Richard Levick fidgets with his laptop, anxious to hear my pitch. In ninety minutes, our flight will land on the island of Antigua. Prime Minister Spencer is expecting us—and a solution. I need to present him with one perfect idea.

The only problem is I have no idea what I'm going to propose. Articles on international trade law are spread out across my tray table. The phrase *cross retaliation* jumps off one page. If someone takes away something dear, you don't just fight back, you take something bigger from them. In chess, when your opponent moves in to take your piece, you don't retreat. You move to take one of their bigger pieces. You go from defense to offense.

In one of the magazines, I read about how, in 1999, American companies were dumping huge quantities of cotton into the Brazilian market, undercutting Brazil's producers. Brazil fought back by manufacturing U.S.-patented AIDS medicine and giving it away for free in Africa. Suddenly, pharmaceutical giants were complaining to American officials about cotton subsidies, and Brazil had restored its market share. All this was sanctioned by the World Trade Organization.

I think about borrowing from Brazil's playbook for Antigua. My strategy has to be adapted to the island's limited resources. And modernized. I leaf through a fat binder of media coverage. By the time we touch down I have a plan.

Levick sees my pen stop scratching and gives me the guarded stare of a veteran PR executive about to field a pitch. It's a look I know well. And my cue to start talking.

"We're going to start a trade war between Antigua and the United States."

Levick huffs like he's caught an elbow to the stomach, but he doesn't kill the idea. My knack for starting fires is the reason he hired me. He wants to hear the rest.

In the current standoff, I tell him, the United States holds the bigger gun. Antigua, by comparison, holds a water gun. We need a third gun. "We create it," I say, "by blackmailing the American entertainment industry."

"Phil, you know we sometimes do business with those people."

"And I hope you don't have aspirations to work for Microsoft."

I go through immigration dressed in a Hawaiian shirt and cargo shorts so the official stamping my passport will believe me when I say I'm on vacation. Levick is still wearing a business suit and gets questioned by immigration officials for fifteen minutes. We walk out of the airport and into a balmy tropical December. We hail a cab, and I call a reporter I know at the Caribbean desk of the Associated Press. If Antigua were about to start a trade war with the United States, I ask him hypothetically, would he be interested in an exclusive? Naturally, I have some terms.

Levick and I face Prime Minister Spencer in a drab conference room. I've pitched presidents, royal families, and dictators in versions of this room all over the world. Spencer is a large man, his hair the shade of white you often see on heads of state.

"Gentlemen, you are aware of our problem," the prime minister says. "What do you propose?"

"I want you to blackmail the United States of America," I tell him.

Spencer grimaces and glares skeptically at Levick. This is par for the course. When presenting a wild idea to a client, you want to give the crazy part first. Then you work backward, and everything else seems reasonable by comparison.

Levick leans forward. "The strategy is more nuanced than that," he says. "Let Phil expand a bit."

I explain to Spencer that in a crisis, sometimes the best strategy isn't to solve the problem. Sometimes it's to make the problem much, much bigger. So big that someone else has to fix it. I tell him that his tiny Caribbean nation has the power to threaten the balance of global economic stability. All they need to do is refuse to honor American intellectual property laws. I tell him about Kim Dotcom's Megaupload, which trades pirated American movies, music, and software and how Antigua could build a similar platform. All the IP from Mickey Mouse to Microsoft Office available for sale at a massive discount on Antigua's national website. The chairman of the Motion Picture Association of America will dial President Obama's office two minutes after the news hits the wire, asking why a gaming dispute in the Caribbean is about to cost his industry billions.

"The U.S. only negotiates with a gun to their head," I say. "I'm giving you that gun."

"And what if America issues a travel advisory on my country?" Spencer asks.

"You were making billions of dollars a year from online gambling. Tourism doesn't bring in that kind of money."

I've got Spencer's attention now. I can see him considering it. "What would my office have to do?"

"You don't have to do anything," I say. "You just have to *threaten* to do it. I'll leak it to the press. Once we have ink, it's real."

"And you can do this with the blessing of the World Trade Organization," Levick adds. "They have already ruled several times in your favor and will approve any sanctions plan you put forward. I'm a lawyer. I'll be able to help navigate the legal weeds on this."

"I know a wire reporter who will want this story as an

exclusive," I say. "If I give him the scoop, he'll run the piece before the U.S. trade representative has a chance to comment."

Spencer leans back in his chair, considers a piece of slate-gray wall above my head. Then he stands and holds out his hand.

I call the AP reporter before I hit the hallway.

Levick and I meet Vincent at the St. James's Club. Vincent adjusts his wide-brimmed hat against the glare of a pink sunset, considering a pair of women doing handstands in the oceanfront pool. An island-hopping political consultant who runs elections in the Caribbean, he has been tasked with making sure our plan doesn't explode Spencer's reelection bid. Vincent's Caribbean-chic wardrobe looks Miles Davis cool next to my cargo shorts, which end halfway down my sunburned shins.

"You're about to set off some big fireworks on a tiny island," Vincent says.

"How else would you threaten the United States?" I ask.

"We need to talk somewhere private," Vincent says. "Not here. Lots of ears listening. I know a place."

The next morning, we push out into the Caribbean Sea on a vessel more raft than boat. Aquamarine water sloshes through the boards of the wooden hull. A bottle of rum rattles around the oars. It's strange to see Richard Levick, a storied constitutional lawyer always dressed for the courtroom, in swim trunks. The ocean eases Vincent's paranoia.

Out here, the only ears that can hear us are those on the red-billed tropical birds and the skipper, who is chain-smoking joints.

"Caribbean politics are hyper local," Vincent says. "A new road is front-page news. If your plan doesn't work, then we're stuck like a fishing boat in a hurricane."

"It's a bit of a long shot, to be sure," Levick says. "Big problems are fixed only by taking long shots. Intimidation is an extraordinary factor in preventing a small country from taking on bullies. We're asking, What if you fought back?"

"Every entertainment lobbyist in DC is going to go ballistic," Vincent says.

"They run on a combination of arrogance and stupidity," I say, bumming a hit from the skipper.

"They make too much money by not taking any risks," Levick says, waving away the joint. "A move this bold will take them by surprise, like Washington sneaking up on the Hessians."

"I've got friends at *TorrentFreak* and other Web-based publications who will champion our side," I say. "They want revenge for the U.S. taking down Kim Dotcom. It'll be like throwing chum to sharks."

"Well," Vincent says, fishing out a bottle of rum. "Cheers to a trade war."

"To a trade war," I say, passing the bottle around the boat.

"My firm represented Guantanamo Bay detainees. Defended people crushed by the Patriot Act," Levick says.

"I have the same feeling now that I did then. In PR, it's rare that one gets to participate as a protagonist of history rather than selling Froot Loops."

"Or bananas," I say.

"Phil, you're the cannon in my orchestra," Levick says, his verbiage loosened by the morning rum. "Many people in this industry think we need first-chair violinists. And we do. But when you're playing Tchaikovsky's *1812*, you really need a cannon."

I stand up and shout "Boom!" over the water.

"Boom!" Levick echoes.

"Boom!"

"Boom!"

I spend the weekend at the St. James's Club, setting up interviews between the AP reporter and Antigua's finance minister. My terms with the AP reporter stipulate an embargo date. He can't go live before midnight Sunday. The timing is crucial. He'll want to be the first to the scoop before it leaks, so he'll publish first thing Monday morning. The U.S. trade representative won't be in their office to return calls over the weekend, and we want the news to hit before they can comment. You win more words for your client if their opposition isn't on the page. Even better if the piece reads, "The U.S. Trade Representative's office did not immediately return an email seeking comment." It makes the opposition look like they're asleep at the wheel. First ink is the most important. Journalism is the first draft of history, and the first story is the first draft of a news cycle. It sets the tone for the coverage.

We're aiming for "David versus Goliath."

Dark clouds roil in the sky over the airport. The terminal is a ghost town. A handful of stranded tourists bicker near the key chain kiosk. I consult the Departures board. All the flights off Saint Martin, where we've just landed from Antigua, have been canceled due to a fast-approaching storm.

"I have to speak at a conference in Houston tomorrow night," Levick says. "We need to get out of here ASAP."

At a bar near our gate, a lone bartender stands polishing daiquiri glasses. I keep him company while Levick calls his fixer, a woman who can find you a town car in Zurich at 3:00 a.m. Levick paces in front of a deserted airport shop filled with carved wooden masks.

"Found a plane," Levick says when he returns to the bar.

"But the airport is closed."

"A private plane."

"Oh, fancy."

A small man wearing a khaki shirt and ripped track pants runs up to the bar. "Hurry, hurry," he says, grabbing Levick's arm and yanking him down the terminal. "They're about to close the runway."

We run through an access door and out onto the tarmac. A light rain has just started. Purple flashes of lightning hit the horizon. We run past grounded jets and jump into a six-passenger prop plane. Inside, I buckle my seat belt and grip the steel seat.

"Is there anything to drink on this flight?" I ask.

"There's an open bottle of rum under your seat," the pilot calls out and starts the propellers.

I fish out the bottle, thank God that it's a handle, and start getting properly anesthetized while Levick fires off emails from his BlackBerry. The plane picks up speed, bumping down the empty runway.

"Can you turn that off?" I ask Levick and nod toward his cell. "I think this may be one of the planes where phones actually jam the radar."

"Yes, don't worry. We have radar!" the pilot calls out, and we take off into the storm.

The tiny plane pitches and rattles as it climbs through mustard-colored clouds. I wait for us to break above the weather, but the plane levels off before we hit blue sky. The clouds turn a deep gray. Fingers of lightning streak by the windows. I count the seconds before the thunder. Two. Maybe three. The rum bottle gets a lot lighter.

This is not good, I think to myself.

"Protagonists of history, right, Phil?" Levick says, gripping my knee.

"Protagonists of history," I say.

The lede of the Associated Press piece reads, "The tiny Caribbean nation of Antigua and Barbuda intends to pursue retaliatory sanctions against U.S. commercial services and intellectual property as part of its David vs. Goliath trade battle with the United States." The exclusive kicks off a storm of coverage in hundreds of papers across the world. Kim Dotcom's contacts at *TorrentFreak* pump the story through the publication's influential Web channels. The internet is firmly on Antigua's side. So are the media. Over the next few weeks, more than a thousand articles are published about the case, applying pressure to the United States to comply with international trade law. An East Asian company that makes animations of major news stories creates one on this dispute.

The story goes viral. "Going viral" is what every client wants, what they pay PR firms to engineer. Here's another secret our industry doesn't want you to know: we have no idea how to do it. Engineering a "viral moment" is like choreographing an earthquake. *If* it happens, it's a shock. And it usually causes damage. Depending on the disposition of the engagement, attention to the wrong aspect of a narrative can be a self-inflicted wound. A lot of PR firms are extremely interested in creating "social media campaigns" and "influencer outreach" to buttress their earned media work. In my experience, you win the mainstream media, and the dog wags its tail: the social media mob follows. There are instances of the tail wagging the dog and social media driving the conversation, but that is the nightmare scenario. That is mob rule.

Just ask Brandon Brown.

Let's fast-forward to 2021. Brandon Brown had just won his first NASCAR race at Talladega Superspeedway in Lincoln, Alabama. When interviewed by NBC Sports journalist Kelli Stavast, Brown said, "This is a dream come true! Wow! Talladega! Dad, we did it!" It should have been the best moment of his life.

Behind Brown, a frenzied crowd chanted, "Let's go, Brandon!" the driver's catchphrase. But hundreds in the crowd were also chanting, "Fuck Joe Biden!" the catchphrase of a good percentage of Americans in 2021. The camera picked up both chants, and the two disconnected phrases fused together. Stavast sealed Brown's fate when she said, "As you can hear, the chants from the crowd—'Let's go, Brandon!'"

"Let's Go Brandon!" became a meme with a potent viral load. Millions of tweets later, the media site TheBlaze was selling T-shirts bearing the phrase. Ted Cruz snapped a picture with a "Let's Go Brandon" sign at the World Series. Kid Rock made it the refrain of his new single. The music video featured Mike Pence in a Photoshopped Nazi armband and a Hitler mustache.

Wanting to depoliticize the narrative for some pretty obvious reasons, Brown hired our PR team. When working on a story of national significance, a good PR executive will try to keep control in the hands of the mainstream media. It's what Proximo says to Maximus in *Gladiator*: "Win the crowd, and you'll win your freedom." In the case of news, the crowd isn't the mob of Twitter users. It's the Associated Press, Reuters, Bloomberg, *Politico*, *Axios*, the *New York Times*, the *Washington Post*, and the *Wall Street Journal*. Get a solid 376 words from each of these outlets, and your client wins.

We contacted Ben Smith, then media columnist for the *New York Times*. Here was an oddity: giving an exclusive interview of a NASCAR racer to a publication that does not exactly have a NASCAR beat reporter. I cannot swear on a stack whose idea it was for the interview to take place *inside* a race car, on a racetrack, but I do remember our firm's advice to Brown: "If you don't like the question, just speed up. He'll either get sick or pass out."

I couldn't have asked for a better headline, "Brandon Just Wants to Drive His Racecar." "But with this meme going viral," Brown told the reporter, "it was more of, I had to stay more silent, because everybody wanted it to go on to the political side. I'm about the racing side." The column demystified Brown as a conservative icon. It showed him to be exactly what he is: a damn good race car driver. We took his image out of the hands of the social media mob.

I've won the crowd for Antigua. Now I need to make sure they don't turn on us. I pitch *USA Today*, a paper with one of the largest circulations in the United States, to publish an op-ed by Antigua's minister of finance. The headline reads, "A Fed Up Antigua Opens Its Doors to Megavideo." I didn't request a shout-out to Kim Dotcom, but I'm happy to see it. The finance minister's piece concludes, "For why should, for example, the U.S. motion picture industry suffer just so the federal government can continue to protect the monopolies of the big American gambling interests?"

The *USA Today* piece lights off another media storm.

This is the appropriate use for an op-ed. Done right, a piece in the opinion pages of a newspaper can operate as a form of track-two diplomacy, one the American media provide free of charge. In an op-ed, heads of state or high-ranking government officials can communicate with each other when other lines of communication are compromised. Unfortunately, most of the op-eds pitched to newspapers are bullshit. People submitting op-eds generally do not know the difference between an op-ed and a "letter to the editor." And many PR clients think that their idea, which might make for a good comment on a social media platform, deserves 650 words in the *New York Times*.

Stop asking your PR people to pitch your op-ed. It won't do any good. It might make you feel better, but unless you are a head of state or a CEO of something massive, the opinion page editors won't give you the time of day. You'll end up published somewhere inconsequential, and you'll be swapping your cash for low-impact billable hours. Remember, an op-ed is *you* saying stuff about *you*. The goal of PR, the brass ring, is to get "earned media," to get a *reporter* to say the right thing about you. That way, people actually believe it.

The Jet d'Eau explodes over Lake Geneva. The water spurt makes me think of the Bellagio fountains when I was babysitting the Doctor. Every time they went off, I jumped a foot. I've come a long way since then. Unlike at BLJ, I now have agency and direction. After ten years in the PR game, I've become an expert at building machines that create useful illusions. I've come to Switzerland to do it again.

Antigua's lawyer waits for me at Mr. Pickwick Pub, just off rue Butini. Tomorrow, he will file legal paperwork at the World Trade Organization headquarters, getting the WTO's blessing to start infringing on U.S. copyrights. The lawyer is an Irishman and an idealist. He can't help but fight for the underdog.

"Going to tell the WTO that, in addition to our website, Antigua will also start selling Manchester United T-shirts," he says.

"Nice touch. Tell that to the reporters," I say. "It will get the attention of the Glazer family."

"Anything else you want me to emphasize to this Reuters lad?"

"Right now, we've created a Mexican standoff between the U.S., Antigua, and Hollywood," I say. "It's time to add a fourth gun."

"Someone who could potentially copycat Antigua's strategy?"

"Who makes the best counterfeit goods in the world?" I ask.

"Ah," the lawyer says. "Let China sleep, for when she wakes, she will shake the world."

"Winston Churchill?"

"Don't be thick. I'd never quote a Brit. Napoleon."

A few pints later, Reuters's Tom Miles enters the bar and shakes hands around the table. "This is the most interesting story to come across my desk in months," he says. "Usually my beat is 'China complains about the U.S. The U.S. complains about China.'"

"This is a 'Man Bites Dog' story," I say.

"More like a 'Fly Lands on Dog' story," Miles says. "Do you think the U.S. will really be worried about Antigua?"

"If they aren't worried enough about Antigua, they should be worried about someone else coming along. If we do something inventive that could pose a lot of problems for intellectual property holders, if we create that precedent, the consequences could be enormous," the lawyer says, launching into a showman routine. "With Antigua, it's twenty-one million. Maybe with China it's going to be twenty-one *billion*."

"Can I quote those numbers?"

"Please do," I say.

The next day, I go with the lawyer to the WTO. I wait in the hall while he files the paperwork for the sanctions. After an hour, he reappears and adjusts his bow tie.

"It's official," he says. "If they didn't think we were serious, they will now."

Days later, we have the blessing of the WTO, and the *New York Times*'s Annie Lowrey declares that the trade dispute between the United States and Antigua is "boiling over."

At a roadside restaurant in Beirut, I watch a bus pull up to the edge of the sidewalk. Families with their entire lives strapped to their bodies step off and wander out to the street where other refugees sit begging for coins. The civil war being waged by my old client Bashar al-Assad has flooded Lebanon with fleeing Syrians. As I wait for Homadi, my driver and fixer, cars whiz by at ninety miles per hour. A wayward van might swerve wrong and end my story right here.

I've come to Lebanon on a mercy mission. One of Levick's pro bono clients is in trouble and needs help. At the demand of Richard Levick, as well as my own conscience, I'm going boots on the ground to help in any way I can. I'm on my own today, as my client has a meeting at the U.S. embassy, a forty-five-minute drive from Beirut. The embassy used to be closer to the city, but on April 18, 1983, a suicide bomber packed over 2,000 pounds of explosives into a truck and crashed the gates. Hezbollah killed sixty-three people and blew one hell of a hole in the building. Since then, the United States has placed its new embassy in a more isolated and defensible position.

Homadi picks me up in a Volkswagen van, and we thunder down Hamra Street until he skids to a stop in front of an apartment complex in Achrafieh, a neighborhood in East Beirut. War reporter Nancy Youssef climbs into the car and starts speaking in Arabic with Homadi. Youssef flew in from Cairo last week; we've shared a bathroom as we've worked our way through Beirut.

Youssef has been lending her investigative efforts to our work, using her network of contacts and fixers like Homadi. Fixers are journalistic Sherpas and are often journalists themselves in their home country. They help reporters navigate social customs, arrange interviews, translate between languages, and keep their eyes and ears open for trends and stories. They always speak English and often come from prominent upper-class families. Like PR pros, fixers often operate behind the scenes. Unlike us, they help uncover stories people in power don't want told.

"They hold your life in their hands, especially someplace like Iraq," Youssef said to me last night at a hookah bar. As she smoked shisha, she told me that when IEDs went off in Baghdad, fixers knew how to move quickly to safe cover. When we reconvene at a Washington, DC, hookah bar a few months later, Youssef will tell me about reporting on Egypt's Rab'a Massacre. She was at the site with her fixer, a Muslim woman, when forces of the Muslim Brotherhood and military police opened fire on protesters in Cairo. Youssef and her fixer fled from the bullets to the gate of the nearest apartment complex, where a man stood guard, refusing to let them inside.

"We're not Brotherhood!" Youssef's fixer implored. "I am a Muslim. You are a Muslim. How can you just let two women sit here and die?"

The man opened the gate, granting them refuge.

"And then we heard the thump of bodies dropping for an hour," Youssef told me. "At the end of the day, I get to leave. And they don't. You want to feel like a coward? Talk to a fixer that's doing this work in the face of jail time."

In Beirut, Youssef and I hound the local media all over

town for leads. Some pay off, but we have not yet achieved our goal. At sunset, Homadi drives us back to the apartment complex. Each time I enter this building, there is the debate: stairs or elevator? The elevator, we are told, often breaks down when the power goes out. For my busted hip, seven flights of stairs are an issue. I roll the dice with the elevator. You might ask, why are we on the seventh floor? An FBI agent once advised me, "You want to stay on floor seven or above in places like Beirut. Most car bombs only have the tonnage to hit the sixth floor or below."

Youssef and I drop our bags on the marble floor of the sparsely furnished apartment. She changes into pajamas, and I dig a few Almazas, Lebanon's national beer, out of the fridge. After days filled with fixers and roadside checkpoints, we steal a moment of normalcy. We head out to the balcony, and I start to spin tales about my days at BLJ. But then I find myself talking about Lindsay.

The next afternoon, I'm having a plate of lahme bi ajeen, a flatbread meat pie, when WhatsApp beeps with a call from a writer from the *New York Times* editorial board. He wants to speak to the prime minister of Antigua. I remember that I am a well-paid flak, not a brave war reporter like Youssef. So, I do my job. When I get through to Baldwin Spencer, I hear calypso music blaring in the background.

"I'm judging a steel drum competition," Spencer says.

"Can you step outside?" I ask. "I've got the *New York Times* on the phone."

After interviewing Spencer, the *Times* editorial board

writes a piece titled "A New Front in Global Trade Wars." "Both sides need to return to the negotiating table and come up with a deal that does not rely on legally approved piracy," they write. I'm still in Beirut when I get a WhatsApp call from Vincent.

"Good news, bad news," he says.

"Good news first."

"Vice President Biden called the prime minister. He says if we make this pain stop, they will settle by the end of the Obama administration."

"How big is the number?"

"Big enough."

"So, what's the bad news?"

"You're fired. You did your job. Antigua doesn't need you anymore. There goes your contract."

In the northern Nigerian village of Chibok, hundreds of girls lie on iron-framed bunk beds in their school dormitory. It is a Monday night in April 2014; tomorrow they will sit for their final math exam. The girls study their textbooks. Go over equations. Some kneel in a prayer room and chant Christian hymns under the light of a full moon. If they pass, they will graduate.

From outside, the girls hear gunfire. Explosions. The school's security guard flees, leaving them alone. Motorcycles and Toyota trucks stop in front of the gate. Men dressed in fatigues and wielding Kalashnikov rifles order the girls to come outside. The girls debate whether they should run. Or pray. They know about Boko Haram. Every girl in Nigeria knows about Boko Haram. The fighters load the girls onto the beds of the trucks, and the trucks drive off into the dark.

I learn about the kidnappings while lounging poolside at a luxury hotel in Dubai where I'm working with a new client. Richard Levick, again clad in swim trunks, has just gotten off the phone with a contact who works closely with Nigerian president Goodluck Jonathan. President Jonathan has been bungling the crisis, getting manhandled by the media. Time for a PR firm to help clean up the mess.

"Well, Phil," Levick says. "Ever been to Africa?"

"I think I'm more useful in DC," I protest.

"They've just transferred us one-point-two million. Do you have all your shots?"

The thought of parachuting into Nigeria in the middle of the Boko Haram kidnappings makes me very thirsty. I approach the poolside bar and ask a man in a linen robe for a bourbon.

"We cannot serve alcohol," he says. "It's a holy day."

"But I'm an infidel."

CHAPTER 8

Goodluck, Phil

Lindsay never cries. Today she can't stop.

"You don't have to go," she says, pulling the car up to the drop-off at Dulles International Airport.

Yesterday, Boko Haram bombed the Banex Plaza shopping mall in Abuja as Nigerians gathered to watch the World Cup. Twenty-two people are dead, and the news is reporting on body parts scattered all over the street. Last night, I received a "heat map" of the district; my hotel is across the street from the blast site. I've had to fill out a "Kidnapping and Ransom" insurance form and make Lindsay the beneficiary of my life insurance policy. I'm not sure how the payout is impacted if I die in a beheading video posted to LiveLeak.

"I'll call you every day," I promise Lindsay. "We have a security detail."

"You don't have to go," Lindsay repeats.

In the boarding queue, I spot Patrick, my flak-in-crime

for the next three weeks. He's stammering into his cell phone. "Yes, love, I know. I know," he says in his hard-to-place accent. Patrick hails from the island of Guernsey, a tax shelter in the English Channel. He ends his call with a hangdog expression.

"I'm going to be a father again," he says. "I just found out this moment."

"Congratulations. You still coming?"

"What's our strategy? My missus will kill me if I come home dead."

"We hop on a plane. Hit duty-free to buy 'gifts' for our clients. See where the job takes us. And get home alive."

You feel Nigeria's heat the minute you step off the plane. It gets under your clothes. Makes itself at home. At the customs desk, four men in black blazers wait in a tight huddle. Our security detail, locals trained by an Israeli security firm with ties to Mossad. A hulk of a man with a shotgun shell–shaped head breaks away from the group. He flashes his fingers over his palms like a blinking traffic light.

"What's your favorite cartoon character?" he asks me.

"Opus," I say, giving my code word.

"Abebi," he says. "Follow."

Patrick grabs my backpack and holds on as we are Sherpa'd at a brisk clip through the steaming airport and into an Isuzu Trooper. In Nigeria, everyone drives fast. Abebi drives faster. Abuja is a blur out the window: street vendors selling vegetables, green-and-white soccer jerseys, kids dodging three-wheeled Keke taxis dusted red. The only object that remains still is the dome of Aso Rock, a four-hundred-meter-tall monolith meditating over the bedlam.

Our Isuzu is slowed by a traffic jam. Abebi lays on the horn as one of our security detail rolls down his window and points an MP5 submachine gun at a hatchback pulled up too close for his liking. The hatchback makes way, and we zip past a complex cordoned off by barriers and surrounded by motorcycle cops guarding blown-out windows boarded up with plywood. Banex Plaza. Looks like they've just finished hosing the blood off the concrete.

"Don't worry," Abebi says. "This part of the city has been pre-bombed. Very rarely do you see two bombings in the same place."

"Pre-bombed," I say. "I've never heard that term before. It's reassuring."

The Abuja Hilton is a fortress. Guards at a checkpoint search our Isuzu for explosives. Another gate, another checkpoint. You quickly get used to seeing guns, noticing them so frequently under jackets and tucked into cargo pants that you forget they are there, that they are everywhere. The Hilton's lobby reminds me of the cantina from *Star Wars* where Han Solo pops Greedo.[*] Petroleum CEOs chat up arms dealers. It's easy to tell them apart. The arms dealers don't have bodyguards.

Patrick and I hit the bar, where World Cup coverage plays

---

[*] Han shot first.

on decade-old televisions. Here waits Noble, a crisis comms mercenary who specializes in parachuting into clusterfucks in Libya, Kenya, and now the Abuja Hilton. The man on the ground for the powers that be.

"My security threw me a handgun when I got in the car," Noble says. "He told me, 'If a car drives up too close, point it out the window. If they don't move within five seconds, unload the clip.' Asked him if I should aim for the tires. 'The windshield,' he told me, the damn windshield."

"Our team had a similar philosophy," Patrick says, gulping a neat whiskey.

"I still have the gun," Noble says. "He never asked for it back."

We're seated beside a group of men from Idaho, potato-fed boys with mustaches and Wrangler jeans. "We've been hired by the Nigerian government to build shooting ranges," says a guy sipping a Bud Heavy. "Train the local military to fight these fucking jihadists."

"How's that going?" I ask.

"These Boko Haram boys play dirty," he says. "But you put a gun in a man's hand. Teach him how to aim it. You give him a chance."

"You'd get along with my friend Preston," I say.

In the waiting room of a Nigerian government building that might as well be called the Ministry of Truth, a series of public service announcements play on a screen. Images of an exploded oil pipeline with dead bodies strewn all about. The words on the screen read, "Pipeline Terrorism Kills." A little different from trying to deter teen smoking, but there you go. Another PSA proclaims: "Corruption Is Wrong" above a giant stack of cash. A bit of a mixed message.

At a security check, a teenager holding an AK-47 demands my backpack. An Opus plush toy, my lifelong traveling companion, falls onto the folding table. The kid steps back. Points the rifle at my chest.

"Hey, calm now," Patrick yelps.

"A toy," I say. "It's just a stuffed doll."

The young soldier considers the level of security threat posed by Opus the Penguin. He lowers his weapon.

Ushered into a room with porridge-colored walls, Patrick and I meet a series of government officials with long, formal titles. Here is their crisis as I understand it.

On the night of April 14, 2014, Boko Haram abducted 276 schoolgirls in Chibok. It is now late June, and while 57 girls escaped on their own, the terrorists still hold 219 girls captive. Boko Haram forced the girls, who are Christians, to convert to Islam and marry their fighters. Cost per bride, six dollars American. The hashtag "BringBackOurGirls" started trending on Twitter. In May, Michelle Obama posted a photo of herself holding up a piece of paper with the hashtag on it, offering the camera lens sad eyes and a pout. Every field journalist with a fishing vest and a Leica descended upon Abuja.

CNN is devoting nightly coverage. Daily press briefings are crammed with reporters asking:

"Why hasn't President Goodluck Jonathan met with the Chibok families?"

"Why does no one in the government know what's happening in the Boko Haram–controlled northeast?"

"Why hasn't Goodluck Jonathan taken military action?"

"Or any action at all?"

"Where *is* Goodluck Jonathan?"

The Nigerians have put out conflicting messages. At one briefing, they said they knew where the girls were being held. The next, they had no idea. They answer in a style I call "totalitarian cryptic." Or tell straight-up lies. It appears as if the Nigerian government were hiding in a clamshell, ignoring the humanitarian crisis dominating world headlines. They've forgotten (or have never learned) Peter Brown's golden rule of PR: "You can't just do a good job. You also have to *appear* to do a good job." Hard fail on both counts. President Goodluck Jonathan needs to change the narrative from "I'm standing idle and letting this atrocity happen" to "We are doing everything we can to #BringBackOurGirls"— before this crisis kills his bid for reelection next spring.

Patrick asks the officials if the Chibok girls are still alive. I ask if the girls are still in Nigeria. The officials respond with bureaucratic vagueness, maddening trails of gobbledygook. They contradict one another. Downplay the crisis. Rule #1 of PR: If you don't know what's going on behind the curtain, you can't tell a story to the media and change the narrative. Without any intel, we can't feed reporters the information we want them to see.

"The whole world just found out where Nigeria is on a map because of these kidnappings," I say. "Everyone is watching you. You need to do something about this problem."

"Problem?" an official asks.

In Nigeria, kidnappings are common. Not the subject of multimillion-dollar lawsuits, national manhunts by the FBI, or made-for-TV movies. Kidnapping is a business here. Hostages are commodities. These officials don't seem to understand or care that the global news media have made the Chibok girls their cause du jour. As I stare at these blathering government men with shiny medals pinned to their chests, I suspect they don't know any more than the nothing they're telling us. We're about to try to play 3D chess with the world media with a set of checkers.

We stand, shake hands, and smile.

The next day, an odd loop begins. A cycle of days that seem possible only in a place like the Abuja Hilton. In the mornings, at the hotel buffet, I drink coffee mixed with honey next to arms dealers. After breakfast, Patrick, Noble, and I jump into Abebi's convoy, the lead car pushing us through traffic. At Goodluck Jonathan's presidential complex, we make suggestions to Nigerian officials. They shoot them down—figuratively, I should specify, given all the guns. Sometimes they take them to a higher-up who shoots them down. Baffled, we put out banal press releases to the local media.

In the afternoons, Patrick calls his pregnant wife. I call Lindsay. Neither is reassured by our dispatches. We watch the World Cup. Argentina's Messi hands the Nigerians a loss. Abebi is apoplectic. We track down priests, scholars, human rights activists, and agents from the Department of State Services, the Nigerian equivalent of Great Britain's MI6. None of their briefs about the situation matches the others. The Hilton buzzes with rumors of suitcases full of money heading to South Africa for arms. Nothing concrete, nothing we can feed to reporters. Just talk that evaporates in the heat. Noble suspects that CIA assets are canvassing the bar. A woman in a crocodile skin dress keeps trying to buy him drinks.

"Honey trap," Noble warns. "Keep a hand over your bourbons."

Around midnight, my cell phone stops working. That means the Nigerian major general Chris Olukolade has arrived at the Hilton. He has a signal-jamming device mounted on the roof of his Land Rover. Patrick sets out dried plantains and a bar cart as Olukolade and his advisors gather in my hotel suite, security details standing sentinel in the hallway. I ask Olukolade what resources they have in the Boko Haram–controlled north.

"Guns, helicopters, soldiers," Olukolade replies.

"No, we don't," interjects an advisor. "You can't tell that to the press."

They are matter-of-fact, but there is no matter to their facts. We stay up most of the night drinking and proposing PR strategies. The light from our room attracts moths big as fists that crash into the glass door to the balcony with dull thuds. The insects hit the glass until it breaks their legs and wings, then flail on the ground, still crawling toward the light.

One night, Olukolade says that Boko Haram is better armed than the Nigerian military.

"Where are they getting their guns?" I ask.

He explains that the government is often late in paying its soldiers, who resort to selling their weapons to Boko Haram to feed themselves.

"You don't have a PR problem," I say. "You have an arms-trafficking problem."

The next day, I head into a hot press room, trying to blend in with the usual faces of shadow brokers lining the back wall. Consultants from Mercury, here to advise the trade minister. Wizards from shops in London and Brussels. Each firm has a different agenda, a miracle tonic to hawk. But they all share a common cause: plunder money from this burning house until it collapses. I sit next to a flak from a British public affairs outfit who does work in dusty places. "Fuck dogs for money" is how Patrick puts it.

Abebi, who follows me like a giant shadow, materializes while a government official dodges questions from CNN. I ask him what he thinks of the official's answers.

"'Ninety-nine lies may help you, but the hundredth lie will hurt you,'" he says. "It is an African proverb."

The next night, the major general and his officials are

back in my hotel suite. We push for Western news organizations to be able to go up to the north of the country. Report on the ground. We offer the officials a local Reuters reporter from Lagos. This will satiate the world press. Give us a visual. They nod and talk among themselves. The next day, nothing happens.

I start to realize that Nigeria might be a *Kobayashi Maru*. In the *Star Trek* movie franchise, the *Kobayashi Maru* was a distressed civilian freighter in a no-win simulation intended to teach fear and humility to new cadets at Starfleet Academy. The simulation had no right answer and would stymie each cadet. Lots of PR clients become their own *Kobayashi Maru*. Some clients could not get a headline if they owned the newspaper. It's the client who is convinced they are front-page news who scares me the most. Their expectations are so out of whack with reality that there is no chance you will ever, ever please them. Fire this client immediately.

Other clients don't understand what news is. It is nothing more complicated than the word *new* made plural. *News*. That's it. It has to be *new*. So, no, I cannot get the *New York Times* to write an article about your press release from last month.

Then there are the clients who just crave seeing their name in the paper. These people are dangerous. With reckless abandon, these clients will go on the record in a heartbeat, refuse any and all media training, and, most important, likely take advice only from themselves or their trusted spouse. I cannot tell you this with enough emphasis: in a crisis, your spouse is not an objective counselor with regard to your public relations needs. They have a vested interest. They are involved.

I try to avoid *Kobayashi Maru* clients. Hard when you're in Africa on a seven-figure job requiring that you entertain evening guests in military getup. The Nigerian administration wants to talk (and pay) its way out of a problem without acting. Richard Levick likes to say, "You cannot talk your way out of something you acted your way into." In hiring us, the Nigerians wanted magicians who would "use their powers'" to will good press into existence. But I am not an alchemist. I cannot turn shit into gold. If terrorists kidnap hundreds of schoolchildren, and you do nothing about it, your PR guy cannot save you. It is as simple as that. If the client does not act, nothing happens. The Nigerians have apparently never learned Newton's First Law of Motion: "Every object will remain at rest or in uniform motion in a straight line unless compelled to change its state by the action of an external force."

Unless God Himself comes down and rescues these girls, I don't know our play. Patrick and Noble are running out of ideas. But then, words of hope start echoing through the Abuja Hilton. You hear them in the chatter of the Idaho gun runners as they smoke their Camel Wides. You hear them in the chlorine-scented halls. You hear them at the pool, where working girls in sarongs make eyes at businessmen two continents away from their wives.

Malala is coming, whisper the denizens of the Abuja Hilton.

Malala is coming.

We no longer need God. We have a chance for a photo op with Malala Yousafzai.

In the world of social activism, there is no bigger celebrity than Malala Yousafzai. After the Taliban shot her in the head for standing up for women's education, Malala became a global icon. The United Nations calls her "the most famous teenager in the world." Wherever Malala goes, the media follow, slobbering.

Patrick and I draft documents that tell President Goodluck Jonathan how he needs to engage proactively to build on the goodwill and the reputation Malala brings to town. Roll out the green-and-white carpet. Malala will be hard on you from day one, we tell his staff. She may look sweet, but she has an agenda. Her comms team are killers. The best in the business, hardened from years at CNN. We can't blow our one chance for a photo op with the golden child of women's liberation. One glittering image turns this whole mess around and kills the narrative that Goodluck Jonathan doesn't care about Nigerian women.

It's better than a photo op with the pope.

Nixon's press aide popularized the term *photo op*. Though dating back to Lincoln, most presidents have used photo ops as a form of "clout chasing" before that was a term. Basically, with a photo op, you want your client to absorb some of the good sentiment inherent in the person with whom they pose for the photo, so that the public connects the two in their minds. (Think Mutassim Gaddafi and Hillary Clinton, if you want the exact inverse of the good of a photo op.) Michael Jordan playing golf with a president, or a human rights activist, or the champion of a spelling bee. That kind of thing.

I have dropped acid only once. But I have to imagine that hallucinating flowers continually bursting into flames for eight hours would have been a lot more normal than December 21, 1970, when Elvis Presley rolled up to the Oval Office carrying a Colt .45 pistol outfitted with silver bullets and demanded a badge from the Bureau of Narcotics and Dangerous Drugs (later known as the DEA). That day, Elvis was named a "Federal Agent at Large" and posed for a photo with President Richard Nixon. To complete the image, Presley was wearing a purple velvet suit and a belt made of gold. Nixon for his part was dressed in a suit, looking somewhat like a regular human.

Each man had good reason to want to appear with the other. The president was riding a high of good approval ratings. He'd promised to end the conflict in Vietnam and racially integrate public schools. Elvis was packing the theater at the Westgate Resort and Casino in Las Vegas and enjoying a resurgence in popularity.

The shot of Nixon and Elvis is the most requested photo from the National Archives. Not the most requested photo of either man but, rather, of any photo *in existence*. It's safe to call it the most successful photo op ever. We hope to re-create some of that magic with a photo of Malala shaking hands with Goodluck Jonathan. Even better if they hug.

A few days before Malala arrives in Nigeria, Levick calls me back to DC.

"I've got the pregnant wife, and *you* get to leave," Patrick says at the bar that night. His nerves are shot after three weeks cloistered inside the hotel. We enjoy the same level of freedom as toddlers. I have to send for my security detail whenever I want snacks.

"Don't fuck up with Malala," I say.

"Buckle up, Buttercup," Patrick says, staring into the bottom of his empty drink.

Lindsay is waiting for me at the airport. I have never been so happy to see another human being. Back at our apart-ment, Darth Vader flops over on his back, demanding to be stroked.

Though I'm back in DC, my head is still at the Abuja Hil-ton. I'm in constant contact with Noble and Patrick as they prep for Malala's arrival and the ensuing media storm. At the Presidential Villa in Abuja, Goodluck Jonathan receives them while reclining on a sofa on a screened-in porch overlooking a manicured lawn filled with statues of giraffes and zebras. As he and Patrick try to impress upon Jonathan the importance of Malala's visit, Noble notices two of the statues come to life. The zebra and the giraffe slowly walk around the lawn. The giraffe shits brown pellets onto the perfect grass.

"What do you think of my zoo?" President Jonathan asks.

"They were so still, I thought they were statues," Noble replies.

"They're very well trained. I've got Michael Jackson's trainer."

On July 12, the Nigerian president's personal driver picks Malala up on the airport tarmac. A motorcade ferries her to the Abuja Hilton with all the pomp and circumstance they'd give a visiting head of state. This is Patrick's doing. Without his guidance, the Nigerians would've let Malala land commercial and be photographed picking up her luggage from a baggage carousel.

It's Malala's seventeenth birthday. Her first trip to Africa. Noble organizes a surprise birthday party with the Chibok families. Malala weeps for the cameras. "It's quite difficult for a parent to know that their daughter is in great danger," she tells reporters. "My birthday wish this year is . . . bring back our girls now, and alive." Malala has done more in ten minutes than the Nigerians have done in three months. *Time* runs the headline "All Malala Wants for Her Birthday Is Safe Return for Boko Haram Girls." She's a hero, to be sure, but as savvy as they get when it comes to PR. Malala wrote the book on childhood activism, and it sold 1.8 million copies.

The next day, President Jonathan and Malala stand in front of cameras for the shot. Patrick is ecstatic. The image goes around the world.

But then Malala speaks to the press, as global activists tend to do.

"I asked the president, is it possible for him to go and see the parents, to see these girls, to encourage them and to tell them that yes, their daughters will return home?" she says, reminding the world that three months after the kidnappings, President Jonathan has yet to receive the Chibok parents, something Malala accomplished before getting over jet lag. She adds that the parents are "hopeless," and "need the president's support." And she warns the Nigerian government: "I will from now be counting days and will be looking."

After a dressing down from Malala, President Jonathan has no choice but to meet with the Chibok parents. Patrick and Noble arrange for a summit at Aso Rock the next day. In the morning, a bus pulls up to the Hilton. The parents refuse to board it. They say they aren't coming. Apparently, an advocate from the BringBackOurGirls movement has gotten in their ears. Told them they are being used as political props. Which, of course, they are.

Patrick calls me in a blind panic. "The president's waiting at Aso Rock with his dick in his hand," he says. "The entire media is there."

There must be a way to spin this disaster. Someone to blame.

"Should I rat-fuck the activists?" I ask.

"Somebody better fuck somebody in the next five minutes," Patrick shouts.

I draft a statement: "Unfortunately, political forces within the Nigerian chapter of Bring Back Our Girls have decided to take this opportunity to play politics with the situation and the grief of the parents and the girls. They should be ashamed of their actions," I write for President Jonathan. "Those who would manipulate the victims of terrorism for their own benefit are engaging in a similar kind of evil: psychological terrorism."

"This is bloody scathing," Patrick says. "Do we really want to call a human rights organization psychological terrorists?"

"Is there any other way to backtrack on a promise to Malala?" I counter.

At Aso Rock, Nigerian officials read the statement aloud to a baffled media. Patrick can't take it anymore and gets on the first plane out of town. In the first-class cabin, he breaks down, sobbing and hyperventilating. "It was the first time I exhaled in four weeks," he tells me.

Three days after Malala's visit to Nigeria, a hashtag goes viral on Twitter. "SomeoneTellLevick" trends for quite some time. "The furious backlash over Washington-based Levick's involvement reflects long-held sensitivity about foreigners who think they know more about Nigeria than Nigerians," writes the *Los Angeles Times*'s Robyn Dixon. "Some accused the firm of profiting from the abductions."

This is what losing looks like:

"PR Firm Under Fire for Contract with Nigeria";

"In Nigeria, Backlash Against U.S. Firm Hired to Improve Image"; and

"Jonathan's PR Offensive Backfires in Nigeria and Abroad."

Not the kind of accolades you submit to the PR industry awards each year.

Other firms have lost worse than this. One of the most fantastic examples of self-immolation is Bell Pottinger. In 2016, the British PR firm was putting up big numbers for some high-profile clients and mining the depths of hell for others. Flaks from the firm went to South Africa, a nation with a slightly complicated history of race relations, and tried to sow racial discord prior to an election. Once this came to light, the media were (rightfully) unforgiving. Bell Pottinger went from making over half a billion on a single contract with the U.S. government to shutting its doors over a single negative news cycle. This was not a case of flying too close to the sun; it was a case of believing you were more powerful than the sun.

Bell Pottinger's time on earth ended in bankruptcy, with creditors fighting over what scraps were left of the firm's ill-gotten gains. Nigeria is a fiasco for Levick. But we don't have to close our doors over it.

A few months after I return from Nigeria, I find Richard Levick in his office. He's sitting under his shelves of law books, going over a stack of press clippings for a potential client.

"This fellow is a murderer," Levick says.

"Wouldn't be the first one."

"I mean, he has actually confessed to the crime. In the papers. Going to have to turn him down."

"Richard," I say, "I've gotten an offer from a polling firm.

They're going to nearly double my salary. I might need money for a ring soon."

"Ah, the money." Levick says. "It's always that, isn't it?"

He strides over to the hollow globe hiding the really good liquor and selects a bottle of Pappy Van Winkle. The same drink I sipped the day Peter Brown fired me. Today, I'm grateful to Peter Brown. Levick hired me because of the skills I had learned at BLJ. Not many people get a chance to learn those skills. Not many people should. But unlike Peter, Levick encouraged me write my own playbook. For the last four years, he has viewed the way my brain works—which most employers would consider a liability—as an asset. "Start with the crazy, I'll rein you in," he always tells me. I grew up at Levick's firm.

"This may be sacrilege," Levick says. "But let's nip it right from the bottle like we did on that fishing boat in the Caribbean. What was our motto that day?"

"Boom."

"Not much chance to be a protagonist of history at a polling firm," Levick says.

"Maybe that's a good thing," I say.

My new desk is plastic, the color of printer paper. My boss tells me to pitch polling data to reporters. "Some really inter-esting trends in these new numbers," he intones. Perhaps I should have expected this at a polling firm. When I call my media contacts, they think I'm joking.

My inbox fills with thousand-slide PowerPoint decks. I

steal glances at my colleagues' screens. They actually seem to be reading all of the slides. At the water cooler, a woman invites me to a birthday party for her dog. He's turning ten. Within hours, I'm bored. Within days, I'm more depressed than when I was working at Mad Mex during college. Within weeks, I'm having panic attacks and am prescribed a truckload of Xanax.

When you put my life down on paper, I have no business being depressed. I'm a senior vice president at one of the best polling firms in the world, making a great salary, living with a woman I love and who loves me back. But there are still days I can't get off the couch. I feel like I'm wearing glasses that filter the world into an alternative reality. No matter how good life appears on the outside, I still feel inside like I'm trapped in hell.

I tell myself I should be happy, which only makes me feel worse—because I can't figure out why I'm not. The more I try to talk myself out of being depressed, the more I spiral. I self-medicate with booze while trying to actually medicate with prescription pills from my doctor. Some drugs cause me to gain weight. Others make my brain feel like it's short-circuiting. I feel as if the doctor is experimenting on me, and it isn't working.

One afternoon, I call in sick and watch *The Empire Strikes Back* with a handle of bourbon for company. Han Solo grins as he pilots the *Millennium Falcon* through an asteroid field, facing down certain death with aplomb. In crisis, he is calm. He is content. I realize that ever since the morning I met Peter Brown, I have been treating my mental illness with crises. Gaddafi, Assad, Qatar, Sarajevo, Dubai (I can't even tell you what happened in Dubai), Antigua, Nigeria. Fifteen years of constant fires, many of which I've lit. With the crises removed, there is no treatment. Except the half-empty bottle at my feet.

When the movie's credits roll, I stagger to a bar three doors down from Camelot, the strip club where I spent my first evening in DC. Most of the dancers from back then have probably moved on to new professions, but I haven't. After my sixth drink, the bartender cuts me off. I come home so drunk I can't speak coherently to Lindsay. I stumble onto the couch, nearly crushing Darth Vader, who hisses and gives me a scratch I can't feel.

"What you're doing to yourself is not okay," Lindsay says the next morning. "I can't fix this. You need to get help."

The thought of losing Lindsay jolts me into action. I get a new therapist. For the first time, I try to talk to someone about my time at BLJ. I tell my therapist I have trouble living with the fact that I covered up for the people who blew up Pan Am Flight 103 and murdered their own citizens with sarin gas. I tell her that when I read books or watch TV, my former clients often appear as the villain in the story. I talk about the terror I felt babysitting the Doctor in Las Vegas and that even though he's dead I still look over my shoulder expecting to see one of his goons. I talk about the fear and the shame. The high I get from taking a risk and coming out on top. I'm finally given a diagnosis: bipolar II disorder with a side of PTSD.

The next morning, I look up relationship statistics for people with bipolar disorder. The titles of the articles scream at me: "When Sympathy's Not Enough, Beating the Marriage Odds"; "Bipolar and Marriage: Can It Ever Work?" The answer seems to be "Not really." One study estimates that around 90 percent of marriages in which one partner has bipolar disorder end in divorce. Bipolar disorder needs a better PR guy. Panicking, I show the articles to Lindsay.

"I've already seen them," she says.

"And?"

"Look, Phil, I'm not with you because you're a safe bet. You're like the bad-guy Forrest Gump of DC. Failing up is your whole thing. At least we finally know what's going on with you. Now we can treat it. We'll figure it out."

I'm silent, too overwhelmed by love that if I try to speak I will weep. I'm a problem. And Lindsay is a problem solver.

"Now take a shower and get to work," she says. "Your feelings made us late."

On a May afternoon in 2015, I ask Lindsay to meet me at the Jefferson Memorial. I take her by the hand and say, "When you realize you want to spend the rest of your life with somebody, you want the rest of your life to start as soon as possible."

Then I ask her to marry me.

To my surprise, quoting *When Harry Met Sally* works, and she says yes.

My first call is to my parents. My second is to Daniel Lippman at *Politico*. The next day, *Politico* puts our engagement into its morning newsletter. It is the first time my name has appeared in a newspaper for something good.

I'm at my desk pretending to read slide 346 of a PowerPoint deck when I see the email. A headhunter looking for a veteran PR operative to represent an Israeli private intelligence agency, Psy-Group. Their motto: "Shape Reality."

"I don't have much info," the headhunter writes. "These guys are ghosts."

Ten seconds later, I'm speed walking down the polling firm's beige hallway, searching for the exit. A coworker in an ill-fitting suit blocks my path.

"You catch that Nationals game last night?" he asks. I can feel his rank coffee breath on my neck.

"Must have missed it," I mumble, sidestepping him and dialing the man who can connect me to foreign spies as fast as my fingers can hit the numbers.

CHAPTER 9

Influence Games

Royi Burstien's pool is swimming with spies. They float on their backs, the water bouncing in the July sunshine. They're smoking endless cigarettes. A hairy-chested operative jack-knifes into the deep end, glides underwater, and pops up near the ladder, splashing me. He climbs onto the deck and tells a joke with the punch line ". . . and then I killed the mother-fucker."

The other spies find this hilarious.

Royi surveys the pool party from a chaise longue. A short, balding man in his fifties, he looks as if he's sat behind a computer for most of his life. The art deco McMansion behind him is all glass and sharp angles. Discount Frank Lloyd Wright on the outskirts of Tel Aviv.

Over the last four days, I've met Royi's family. Heard what he wants me to hear of his story. After fifteen years running psychological operations for the Israel Defense

Forces, he decided to repurpose his military skills in the private sector. What better way than to assemble top-level former Mossad agents and military intelligence officers and sell their skills to anyone with a checkbook?

Yesterday, I entered Psy-Group's offices through an unmarked door. Inside the bland building, operatives typed behind computer screens. They wore jeans and thick beards. Many were in their mid-twenties. "Royi picks us up at the gate of the IDF when we leave the military" is how one agent described his recruitment.

Psy-Group works in color-coded teams. Red, Blue, and Green gather intelligence. Rubik team, a blend of colors, is a hybrid of intelligence gathering and influence campaigns. Psy's bread and butter is to create false online identities called avatars. These avatars extract intelligence on targets, usually enemies of Psy-Group's clients. When it needs to, the firm brings these avatars to life using real-world operatives. For "Project Madison," a virtual honeytrap for jihadists, Psy created a Facebook page for an all-American girl named "Madison" who was interested in converting to Islam. It then used "her" to infiltrate ISIS groups in need of Muslim brides.

Royi's spies don't look like secret agents from movies. Nobody has a watch that shoots laser beams or shows me their pen gun. But they have some tells. The operatives move methodically, never in a hurry, exceedingly aware of their surroundings. Even while sunning their hairy bellies pool-side, they scan for exit routes. They speak slowly, asking me questions, prompting me to tell them about my work for

Gaddafi. After a few conversations, they know much more about me than I know about them.

At the pool, Royi feeds his dog a scrap of shawarma from the grill. He tells me he has aggressive aspirations for his intelligence firm. Psy-Group will be a better Black Cube, he tells me, referring to a competing Israeli intelligence outfit. He wants to pitch Project Madison to the U.S. State Department. Psy's avatars have extracted useful intel on ISIS fighters, which Royi views as proof of concept to generate high-level clients. That's where I come in. I'm to tap my extensive network of Washington contacts.

Before I leave Israel, Royi gives me a promotional brochure. The cover features a cat casting the shadow of a lion and the message "Reality is a matter of perception." Some services offered are euphemistic, such as "Targeting & Monitoring." Read: surveillance. Others, more to the point, like the "Honey Traps" advertised on the second page.

"What do I say when people ask about the legality of all this?" I query.

"Everything we do is legal in the jurisdiction in which we do it."

"I'll use that line."

"You know what you need to do in the States," Royi says. "Now go do it."

And with that, I'm Psy-Group's representative in DC.

When you work for spies, unexpected things appear in your inbox. Documents in myriad languages, satellite photos of houses in Middle Eastern countries, memes in Hebrew, photos of cats in war zones. When I was "interviewing" in Israel, Royi asked how many languages I spoke. At Georgetown, I received a "gentleman's C" in Spanish, on the promise that I would not take the next level.

One day, I receive compromising audio files of a prominent South African family who made their fortune selling skin-lightening cream to Black South Africans during apartheid. On the tapes, the family members bad-mouth one another. Lob accusations of greed. I'm to weaponize this intelligence by putting it into the hands of reporters from around the world. Make sure the targets of Psy's investigations appear in the international news. Turn information into influence.

"Who is this for?" I WhatsApp Royi.

Psy-Group can't reveal its client. Just a code name. All I'm told is the headline Psy wants—and that I'm to crush the family. Perhaps get the press to mention that they opened an apartheid museum.

I'm about to break one of my rules of PR: "Know your customer."

No such requirement exists in the field of public relations. Normally, this rule is reserved for banking or financial services. Financial institutions need to know their client's identity, suitability, and the risks involved in maintaining a business relationship with them. As you can imagine, many such regulations came about after 9/11. To combat financing of terrorism, banks around the world had to know a little bit more about their customers before legally laundering their money.

But that's just a "know your customer" requirement. Ideally, you should also know your customer's customer. The person actually paying the bills. Impossible when you work for an organization of former Mossad spooks. I don't know who owns Psy-Group.

Additionally, I need to keep in mind the law of unintended consequences. Every time you place a story, there is some collateral impact. (I use the word *impact* here because sometimes news coverage helps the innocent, but often the word *damage* is more appropriate.) But if you don't know your paymaster, you can't know their motives. So you can't know who they are trying to hurt with this particular headline. If collateral impact damages one of their associates, you are putting yourself in danger.

If I break my first rule, I'll be forced to break another. I'm always up front with journalists about my clients' identity. In this case, I can't be. You lose a lot of credibility with reporters when you won't divulge the source of your income.

I pitch international reporters from *Forbes* and the Associated Press, steering clear of the American press. In order not to trigger any obligations under the Foreign Agents Registration Act, I'm doing my best to avoid even inadvertently influencing reporters or disseminating information to reporters in the United States on behalf of a foreign principal.

The reporters ask for the source of the recordings. I say,

"Not for attribution," which translates to "They fell off the back of a truck." But this works only if the journalist knows the source. Reporters are willing to keep certain facts from their readers, if they know said facts. A note to journalists who are offered this kind of intel: walk away. If someone you barely know comes to you with information and they don't know its provenance, it's probably a trap.

"This seems sketchy," the *Forbes* reporter tells me. "Doesn't meet our journalistic standards." The AP doesn't return my email. The reporters run in the other direction.

I don't.

I'm newly married, Psy-Group keeps the lights on, and I'm mastering the art of influence brokering. Lindsay and I get a small country home on the Eastern Shore of Maryland. More important than the money is the thrill of the work and treating my depression with risk-taking behavior. My bipolar lows feel like a free fall from an airplane without a parachute. Working for Psy-Group feels like skydiving.

In December 2016, shortly after Trump defeats Hillary Clinton, Royi and I down a few bottles of lunchtime vino alongside Alexander Nix, CEO of Cambridge Analytica. Royi swoons over Cambridge Analytica's ability to influence elections, his highest aspiration. Super PACs are cash cows, teats ready to be suckled.

Nix, in turn, is obsessed with Psy's cloak-and-dagger tactics. Royi says Psy-Group has the capacity to create a large number of highly credible avatars. Enough to man a human resources or staffing agency. Psy's staffing agency creates hundreds of fictional job postings tailored to targets of an intelligence operation. They advertise the job postings over LinkedIn.

"Creates less suspicion if the target comes to you," Royi says, rolling his *r*'s, a feature of his thick Israeli accent.

When the target applies for the job, the intelligence gathering begins. Dangle a high salary and good benefits in front of someone, and they are often willing to discuss their former and current employers. Sometimes, they'll even send proprietary information from their company. Sometimes they accept free travel to a foreign country—ideal for a covert recording of them being "interviewed" by the avatar. During this interview, a real-world operative extracts more information from the target.

LinkedIn is Psy-Group's first line of offense. The fastest way into the living rooms and lives of their targets. If LinkedIn is Psy's first stop, governments are doing this too. Be careful who you accept on LinkedIn.

Nix can't get enough of Royi's tales of espionage.

"Black Cube rented a hotel room to spy on the chief prosecutor at Romania's National Anticorruption Directorate," Royi says, eager to bad-mouth a rival outfit. "Armed agents caught them red-handed. Everyone went to jail. Idiots! We'd never get caught doing that."

Royi doesn't say Psy-Group wouldn't try to hack a government, just that it wouldn't get caught.

Good enough for Nix. Psy-Group and Cambridge Analytica

sign a memorandum of understanding and pitch Project Madison to the U.S. State Department. They want the United States to sponsor a larger version of Madison to dig into anti-American propaganda sponsored by China, Iran, and Russia.

Over the next months, I will introduce Psy-Group to my entire network, conducting well over one hundred introductory meetings with PR, lobbying, law, and security firms. I hand out Psy's brochure to every political consultant with an expense account. Almost every segment of the DC influence infrastructure meets with Psy-Group.

Royi wants to meet in the underground dining room hidden behind a false wall at PJ Clarke's in DC. He orders a steak and fills me in on his latest intelligence op, "Project Butterfly." Psy has been gathering kompromat on university activists backing the Boycott, Divestment, Sanctions (BDS) movement and leaking it to social media through avatars. Objective: defame, fracture, plant seeds of conflict.

"Anyone can gather intelligence," Royi tells me, neatly slicing chunks of beef. "We want to influence the way people think. Place thoughts we want them to have in their minds."

"Sounds like my job."

"We have fewer limitations."

Royi and I have grown close. Not quite friends. Rather, we have mutual respect based on each one's fear of the other. I fear Royi's ability to manipulate reality in the shadows; Royi fears my ability to make anything public to the world at a moment's notice. We talk almost every day over WhatsApp. Though he's a spy, he's one of the most disarming clients I've ever had.

When the bill comes, Royi hands me a silver laptop. "Keep this locked in a drawer and running at all times in your office," he says.

I don't ask questions. Royi operates on a need-to-know basis, telling me just enough information to let me do my job.

I head to the DC WeWork office of Chester Creek Consulting, the boutique PR firm I founded eight months ago. Chester Creek Consulting has two clients on retainer: a polling firm and Psy-Group. I plug in the laptop, and it whirs to life. I lock it in the bottom drawer of my desk and try to forget it exists.

A few days after Royi gives me the laptop, I throw Psy-Group a networking party at Old Ebbitt Grill, a classic DC haunt just steps from the White House, to announce the opening of its new office—which is really just my WeWork. Friends from the Middle East Institute sip cocktails with international spies and reporters from *BuzzFeed* and the *Hill*. *Politico*'s newsletter *Influence* writes up the party in its Spotted section and *poof*, Psy-Group has officially arrived in Washington.

Then things take a turn.

Royi has begun to move Psy-Group's money through my bank account. "It's easier for clients to pay an American account. Just generate an invoice from Chester Creek for one hundred fifty thousand," he explains, and he WhatsApps me a routing number for a bank in Cyprus, where Psy-Group is apparently headquartered—at least on paper.

"Why are you based in Cyprus?" I ask.

"We have clients in the Gulf States," he says. "They really don't like wiring money to Israel."

Another request comes in short order. This time, tens of thousands bound for an account in the Seychelles. I'm told to generate an invoice for a consulting company. When the money appears in my account, I feel like I'm back in Vegas, handling Mutassim Gaddafi's shrink-wrapped cash. Once again, I'm dealing with very serious people capable of doing very serious things, so I don't ask questions.

I make so many trips to the bank that I become chummy with my banker Greg, a living incarnation of a Ken doll. You can see his delts bulging under the shoulder pads of his suit. "You are by far my most interesting client," Greg comments, but he seems otherwise incurious about the fortunes I'm moving to tax havens around the world.

One day, I come in wearing a stained button-down and cargo shorts. Seventy-five thousand dollars has been freshly deposited into my account. "I need to send a wire to the West Bank," I tell Greg.

"Can we do that?"

"Check for the West Bank in your system. If it's there, it must be okay."

"That sounds right," Greg says, flashing a gigawatt smile. "I'm not seeing a West Bank, but Palestine is an option."

"That'll work."

"All set," Greg says. "Seventy-five thousand dollars sent to Palestine. Anything else I can help you with?"

"You need to be careful," Lindsay warns when I come home.

In July 2017, Royi pops up in DC without warning. Lately, he's just started to appear, like a jump scare in a horror flick. Royi wants to meet up at an Italian restaurant on K Street. As always, I'm twenty minutes early. Royi is already waiting.

"Do you have your laptop with you?"

"Right here."

"Get it out."

Royi tells me to generate three hundred thousand dollars in invoices to an entity with an almost comically shell company–sounding name. I'm to transfer the funds to an account number that he will WhatsApp to me after the invoices clear. When he gets up from the table to use the restroom, I text my accountant.

"Danger, Will Robinson," she replies. "Don't do this."

I inform Royi that I can't move his three hundred large. It would tip the funds that Psy-Group has run through my account to over a million dollars, a threshold that would alert regulators.

"Smart," Royi says. "We'll find another way."

Later that month, I get an email from Royi. I open the attached PDF, titled "Project Rome." The document explains that *if* Psy-Group had been engaged by the Trump campaign to influence the 2016 presidential election, this is how the firm *would* have done it. It would have covered its tracks better; and it wouldn't have gotten caught.

I remember that in December 2016, shortly after Trump won the election, Royi asked me to set up meetings with both the Republican and Democratic National Committees to pitch them on swaying elections. Lindsay vetoed the idea, citing, among other things, its likely illegality, and I declined.

I archive the Project Rome email, but I don't set up any meetings.

A week later, I get a WhatsApp message from one of Royi's minions. He has many of them. "A package is going to arrive for you," he says. "Bring it to Nine-two-three Sixteenth Street. Give it to a man named Joel Zamel."

Like clockwork, my phone bings. My apartment building's front desk has a FedEx package for me. Big enough to contain a hard drive. I smoke a joint on my roof before hitting the streets of DC. I could do this walk blindfolded, under the influence or sober. I know the pace I need to keep to hit each traffic signal as it changes to "Walk." DC is like a giant park lined by office buildings. The architecture is a mix of beautifully constructed neoclassical and modern works of stone and concrete. Other buildings, constructed during grimmer architectural eras, are ugly eyesores that will one day be replaced in the District's constant reconstruction. I pass Archibald's, a strip club where Hunter Biden was once a frequent guest.

On Sixteenth Street, I enter the St. Regis hotel, the effects of the joint still working. It dawns on me that I don't know what Zamel looks like. I do a Google Image search for "Joel Zamel" on my cell. Nothing. Guy is a ghost. I fidget with my phone, looking up the history of the St. Regis. Just as I thought. In 2015, the St. Regis hotel was sold to Al Rayyan Tourism Investment Company, based in Qatar, for an undisclosed amount of money.

I'm quite stoned. In a hotel owned by interests aligned with my former client Qatar. Waiting on an Israeli spook. Holding a package I haven't opened.

I jump when I hear someone say my name. Behind me stands a balding middle-aged man with a dark beard. I hand over the package. He nods and disappears into a bank of elevators.

In a library on the Eastern Shore of Maryland, I look over my shoulder. Behind me, an old man in a bowling shirt reads a large-print Jeffrey Archer novel called *Be Careful What You Wish For*. On a weekday at noon, we are the only patrons. Good.

The old Dell computer in front of me chugs to life. I create the Gmail address 733X@gmail.com and WhatsApp it to a Psy-Group agent. A document pings through. I print it out. The cover sheet is written in Hebrew. Or Arabic. I try not to look too closely before sealing the document in a manila envelope. The less I know, the better.

This isn't my first time doing this. Or even my fourth. Royi and I have a system. He WhatsApps a cryptic note, and I leave DC. I drive ninety minutes out to a little town in Maryland with a farmers' market and sandwich shops that brine their own pickles. In the public library, I fire up one of their "white" (but rather dirty) computers to generate a burner email address. I use my old phone numbers, changing one digit. I message Psy-Group the email address. They send a document. I print it out. Or I save the file to a flash drive fresh out of the packaging. One use only. Then I close the email, clear the cache, delete the history. I'm instructed not to write down the log-in credentials for these email accounts. Forget they happened. This works. Under penalty of perjury, I could not tell you a single one of those email addresses or passwords. Then I deliver the package to wherever Royi needs it to go.

Today, as I head for the library's exit with the most recent printout in an envelope, my phone buzzes with a WhatsApp message. An address in Foggy Bottom. I drive east, doing the speed limit. As I cross the bridge over the Chesapeake Bay, the landscape opens into giant, flat prairies of blue water. A waddle of waterfowl beat their wings, flying south toward the Blackwater Wildlife Refuge.

Driving, I think about the old man at the library reading his novel. My father loves Jeffrey Archer and gave me his books to read when I was a teenager. Archer chronicles the follies of media barons and he once hosted Peter Brown–style parties at his penthouse, giving journalists instructions on how to find the bathroom: "Go past the Picasso, left at the Matisse." Archer has had a life worthy of his own pen. His father was a bigamist con man who hoodwinked New York City's upper crust. In his youth, Archer was a world-class runner, winning the highest honors at Oxford. Later on, he served as a member of Parliament and as a confidant to then prime minister Margaret Thatcher. After leaving government service, he fell on hard times and published his first bestseller just after he was declared bankrupt. When one international bestseller followed another, he became quite wealthy and involved himself with a charitable organization investigated by authorities. In the witness box, Archer denied an allegation that turned out to be true. He has lived a life of highs and lows. A life, like Peter Brown's, that I lionized in my youth. Then I remember that the court sentenced Archer to four years in prison for perjury. And that I'm thirty-nine.

An hour later, I pull up to an office building made of steel. I've never been here, which is unusual. When you've been in DC as long as I have, you've been in every building. Envelope in hand, I'm buzzed through a locked door. Then a second door. A fellow with a gun on his hip approaches.

"Are you Phil?"

"Yes."

"Then that's for me."

He takes the envelope. I head back out into the street and try to put the errand out of my mind.

Lindsay is still in her pajamas when the FBI calls. It's February 8. Six thirty in the morning. As I listen to the agent on the other end of the line, I look at my wife. I've just brought her coffee, as I do every morning. She likes it with a splash of cream. Her face is focused, her fingers shooting off the morning's emails. This is the last image I'll have of her before I have to tell her that our lives are about to change forever. I savor it for a moment before I speak.

"Lindsay, the FBI is downstairs," I say. "They will be up in one hour. You need to leave."

Lindsay looks at me as if I'm joking. It's the kind of joke I would tell. But it's real.

Knock.

Knock.

I'm standing in my kitchen, staring at the door. I know what's on the other side of it.

Knock.

Knock.

Knock.

I open up to find a man and a woman wearing pistols on their hips. The woman steps forward.

"Mr. Elwood, I'm Agent Logan from the FBI," she says. "Is now a good time?"

In February, night falls early. I'm sitting in the dark when Lindsay comes home. She switches on a lamp, casting our bedroom in dim orange, and sits cross legged on our bed. Tries to take a breath but comes up short. She concentrates hard on breathing, trying to get enough air into her lungs.

"It's been happening all day," she tells me. "Every time you messaged, I had to run to the bathroom to try to breathe. It's not like I could tell my boss about the situation."

"I'm so sorry," I say. Seems like a good place to start.

"Phil, we always tell each other everything," Lindsay says. I watch her throat muscles constrict. "Tell me everything."

The FBI agents divulged nothing to me. They weren't there to provide information; they were there to extract it. I had a pretty good idea which client the FBI was interested in. Agent Logan did most of the talking. She asked ninety minutes of questions.

Who owns the Psy-Group?

Royi Burstien.

Where was the Psy-Group incorporated?

Cyprus, for geopolitical reasons, as far as I knew at the time.

"Do you know any of that for certain?" Lindsay interjects.

"They acted like I was giving a lot of wrong answers. I only know what Royi tells me. He speaks in puffs of smoke."

"Right, because you work with . . ."

"Spooks who don't exactly read me in. The FBI were really interested in something called Project Rome. I said I had no clue. And they asked about someone named Joel Zamel. I don't know a Joel Zamel."

"No, no, no," Lindsay says. "You do. His name was on a package in our house. That you delivered . . ."

"To the St. Regis," I say, suddenly recalling the shadowy figure disappearing into the elevator bank. A firecracker of anxiety crackles in my stomach.

"Holy shit," Lindsay says. "You told the FBI you didn't know him?"

"I told them what I remembered."

For a split second, Lindsay laughs, taking her first full breath of air. "Yeah, because that's something normal people forget, Phil."

"They asked for the last two and a half years of my emails. Phone records. Bank records. Text messages. WhatsApp messages."

"Oh God, the bank records."

"That's when I said I needed to talk to a lawyer."

"That's how you should have opened the meeting."

"Right," I say, because she is right, a fact that has become stunningly obvious.

"You need to call a lawyer now."

I'm dialing before Lindsay finishes her sentence. David Saltzman picks up on the first ring. I've been friends with Saltzman for ten years. He received my first-ever subpoena, when I worked for a very misunderstood organization. I explain the current situation. He gives me some advice as a friend.

"You need more than friendly advice right now," Lindsay says as soon as I hang up.

Sixty seconds later my phone rings.

"You don't need a friend," Saltzman says. "You need a lawyer."

Indeed I do.

The prosecutor assigned to my case is Zainab N. Ahmad, a counterterrorism specialist. I read a *New Yorker* profile on her with the subhead "Zainab Ahmad Has Prosecuted

Thirteen International Terrorist Suspects for the American Government. She Hasn't Lost Yet." According to the piece, Ahmad has spent more hours questioning al-Qaeda than any other American prosecutor.

"Do they think you're a terrorist?" Lindsay asks.

"This is not good," I say, visions of black bags and Guantanamo Bay dancing in my head.

"No, this can't be right," Lindsay says, and does a deep dive into Google. "Hold on," she says. "She's one of Robert Mueller's new senior prosecutors."

For a very brief moment, we are relieved. I've been caught up in the Mueller investigation. At least I'm not the target of a counterterrorism unit.

Then reality hits. Lindsay is working as the chief spokesperson for a leading university. She is terrified that her colleagues or friends from the Clinton world think tank she has just left will discover any connection with Mueller. Her credibility could be in peril by association.

"You need to fix this," Lindsay says.

CHAPTER 10

Target or Source

Agent Logan escorts me through the halls of WeWork. I flash-back to being frog-marched into the back of a police van and handcuffed to the floor at twenty-one years old. Today, I suspect I am in much, much more trouble. A drunken indiscretion is easier to forgive than being a bagman for a cadre of foreign spies caught up in the Mueller investigation.

We reach my office, a single desk behind a glass door. I keep nothing at this desk. No photos of Lindsay or Darth Vader. No personal effects of any kind. I open the desk drawer and show the FBI agent the silver laptop, still whirring away. Agent Logan unplugs it and places it in an evidence bag. She hands me a receipt as if I've just bought a cup of coffee, rather than handed over contraband likely brimming with evidence useful to the FBI. This is the last time I'll ever set foot in this office.

"Come on," Logan says, "I'll drive you home."

"Do I get in the front seat or the back?"

"Up front. You're not under arrest, and this is not an Uber."

"At least you got to ride up front," Lindsay offers when she arrives home from work. She looks exhausted. Hasn't been sleeping through the night. "Did Agent Logan ask why you made them wait an hour the morning they showed up?"

"She was kind enough not to bring it up," I say. "But we're not exactly chummy. Today we had a three-hour meeting previewing my evidence at Saltzman's office. She wasn't happy when I mentioned the Psy-Group gave me a laptop."

Lindsay looks shocked. "You hadn't told her this before?"

"Two-plus years of Royi's weird shit. I'm going to forget some details," I say.

Lindsay has a point. When I recalled the laptop, Agent Logan had the same look on her face as Lindsay does now. Her demeanor changed, as if she believed I had been hiding something—the last thing I want her or Lindsay to suspect.

"I am giving them everything," I say. "We spent all day dissecting every email, WhatsApp, and bank transfer."

"Sometimes the story you tell isn't quite the whole story," Lindsay says. "This time, make sure it is."

I feel like my testimony in front of Lindsay is a dry run for Mueller's people. I've been subpoenaed by the Office of Special Counsel and will soon have to explain myself in a formal interview. But it's more important than anything I will tell the government. I can stomach jail, maybe. I can't stomach losing Lindsay.

* * *

A week later, my lawyer, David Saltzman, and I arrive at a concrete-colored Department of Justice office at 395 E Street Southwest. We surrender our phones at security and are ushered into a small interview room by Zainab N. Ahmad herself. Ahmad has dark hair cropped at her shoulders and brown eyes that cut right through you.

While prepping for this interview, Saltzman told me, "Phil, you make a much better witness than a target." I'm only too eager to heed his advice and have supplied the FBI with the last two and a half years of my emails, phone records, and text messages. It's the same strategy I've used to keep my name out of the news. Whenever a reporter threatens to include me in a story, I become a source, offering new information in exchange for anonymity. Prove your worth, and you stay invisible. Today, I'm doing it to stay out of federal prison.

Ahmad questions me for four hours about Psy-Group. The trip to Israel. The hundreds of thousands of dollars moved through my account to Cyprus. She has questions about the laptop, which likely generated avatars from a server protected by a virtual private network.

"Did Royi Burstien ever tell you about pitching Trump's camp an election influence campaign called Project Rome?" Ahmad asks.

I have the "If We Did It" email about Project Rome, a PDF marketing brochure that was essentially Psy-Group's explaining how it could have swung the election for Trump if he had hired them. But a meeting with the Trump Organization is news to me, and I fear it will be newsworthy to reporters. Saltzman lawyers me through the interrogation, ensuring I don't perjure myself. Ahmad wants to know if I'm still working with Psy-Group. I answer truthfully, telling her that I terminated our agreement the day the FBI knocked on my door.

I walk out of the Department of Justice's makeshift offices a free man, thanks to Saltzman's lawyering. But the ramifications of being a Mueller witness extend far beyond the justice system. I've introduced Psy-Group to my entire DC network, every reporter and government contact I spent a lifetime cultivating. Now I'm clientless, and gossip about my connection to the Mueller investigation has hit my business prospects. I've become radioactive in Washington. No new business is coming in to Chester Creek until this blows over. And that's not happening anytime soon. Mueller's investigation is a black cloud of suspicion swirling over DC, darkening every aspect of my life.

"I don't have anyone to talk to about this," Lindsay vents that night while furiously constructing a cat tree for Darth Vader in our living room. "I haven't told any of my friends. I haven't even told my parents. I'm texting cat GIFs to the Ladies' Lounge like nothing is wrong."

The "Ladies' Lounge " is a group chat for Lindsay's excessively high-performing female friends, all liberal communications professionals with ties to DC. They discuss everything. New gadgets, locations for happy hour, and the ups and downs of their lives. Nothing is spared. Except this.

"It's not like I can text, 'Guess what? My husband might have helped spies overthrow democracy,'" Lindsay says, stacking the cat tree's parts into neat piles. "They won't find it charming. People are scared of what's happening to our government, Phil. And angry. I'm not like you. I can't bottle up my secrets and drink them down at Commissary."

"Hey."

"Sorry. That wasn't nice," she says, sitting on the floor. "I'm just—ugh, why are these fucking instructions written in pictures?"

"Did the thing where you can't catch your breath happen at work again today?" I ask.

"Phil, it happens every day," Lindsay says. "When I can breathe normally, I'll let you know."

I try to stick artificial leaves onto the cat tree's plastic trunk. The Xanax I've been taking blurs my coordination, and I fumble, snapping one of the branches.

"Just let me do it," Lindsay says. She stares up at me from among the parts of the half-constructed cat tree, giving me a suspicious look I've come to know too well. "Did you know anything about the Psy-Group meeting with the Trump campaign?" she asks, built-up anxieties tumbling out into the open.

"I swear to you I didn't."

It's the truth. But that doesn't make things any easier on Lindsay. Every target of the Mueller investigation gets washed out in the press a few months later. If my name appears in print, it will blowtorch the smoldering remains of my career.

"Everything will be fine," I tell her.

But I have no idea how any of this can, or ever will, be fine. I'm profoundly sad that my risky behavior has made Lindsay feel she's in jeopardy. FBI agents knocking on the door before breakfast is not a normal marital hiccup.

Lindsay tries to think of ways to solve or at least control the situation while I lie on the couch, paralyzed by anxiety. I'm waiting for a story with my name in it to drop on the front page of the *Washington Post.* A headline runs through my mind: "Former Gaddafi Flak Helps Israeli Intelligence Firm Manipulate American Democracy." "Phil Elwood" will no longer be a dead jazz reviewer from San Francisco. I'll be one Google search away from my worst mistake and forever unemployable. In my line of work, anonymity is priceless. PR people operate in the shadows by design. I'm paid to be the man behind the curtain, not the sideshow on the stage. If that happens, I'll become a problem not even Lindsay can solve.

Mueller's subpoena strongly suggests that I tell no one about this investigation. But anonymity is earned. Not given. My connection to Psy-Group is a bomb that will go off at some point. If I provide valuable intel to reporters, I could keep my name out of the press and control, to some extent, whether the ensuing explosion kills me or someone else.

The sign on the door of Morton's reads, "Proper Attire Required." I haven't shaved, showered, or changed my cargo pants in a week. The maître d' is kind enough to give me a table on the enclosed patio, the only place in DC where you can smoke with your steak. I start filling the ashtray. In the smoking section, the TVs are tuned to Fox News for the lobbyists chewing on cigars; inside the restaurant, MSNBC plays for the think tank set. Both networks have tunnel vision: *Mueller, Mueller, Mueller.*

I'm a nervous wreck. Lindsay and I argued last night, and I got up at 4 a.m. I've been pacing a circuit between my roof, the marijuana dispensary, and my bed. I suck up half a pack of Camels before Byron Tau arrives. Tau, a reporter, covers the Hill from across the street at the *Wall Street Journal*.

"This one is really bad," I say.

"Figured. Haven't heard from you lately."

I've given Tau lots of leads over the years. He knows I don't waste reporters' time. We met when he worked as Ben Smith's assistant. It was Tau who ghost-wrote the "World Cup vs. Gym Class?" piece under Smith's byline.

"Everything I'm about to tell you is off the record," I tell Tau and make sure he affirmatively agrees.

"Off the record" is a two-way contract. On September 16, 2021, *Politico*'s newsletter *West Wing Playbook* had the lede "Before *Washington Post* columnist Jennifer Rubin became one of the most reliable defenders of the Biden administration, she was one of the Obama administration's most reactionary critics." The piece described how when *Politico* reached out to Rubin and her employer, the *Washington Post*, for comment on this headline, Rubin fired off one of those emails you should save to Drafts. The subject line: "OFF THE RECORD." *Politico* stated: "Since we never agreed to conduct such an off-the-record conversation, we are publishing [Rubin's email] below in full." I won't restate what you are free to google yourself, but it was not the columnist's finest hour. If a reporter doesn't affirmatively agree that a conversation is off the record, it isn't.

After Tau orders the truffle fries, I push my phone across the table and let him read my subpoena from the Special Counsel's Office.

"Holy shit," he says.

I fill him in on the last two years of spy games. He licks his reportorial chops when Mueller enters the story. The special counsel's investigation is the biggest news story in Washington. Tau's editors are breathing down his neck for any incremental development in the Mueller investigation, and frankly, the *Journal* is getting beaten every day by its crosstown rivals at the *Washington Post* and the *New York Times*. Tau is under heavy pressure, and the opportunity to reveal more about the strange path Mueller is treading is tantalizing.

"I've been spending eighteen hours a day standing in the hall outside Hill meetings in the hope of getting some House Intelligence Committee member alone for five minutes to try to get them to give me a tidbit of information," Tau says. "I want to be ahead of this story."

My next meeting with Tau is at Joe's Stone Crab. I'm glad to have a meal on the *Journal*, given that I haven't worked in two months. Tau has been doing his homework. He knows who owns the Psy-Group: Joel Zamel, the man to whom I handed a package at the St. Regis. Tau has spoken to Zamel's lawyer. He is in reporter mode, ready to grill me for hours. He wants to harvest primary source documents from my laptop.

"If we do this," I say, "I've got to remain anonymous."

"I figured as much," Tau says.

"My reasoning here is clear," I say. "I'm informing on former Israeli spies. I fear many things from them, including reprisals. Keeping my name secret is paramount to my safety."

"Fair."

To structure an anonymity deal, you need a monopoly on the information a journalist wants. Check. Or you can position yourself as the second source confirming information they already have but cannot print without confirmation. I'll also be helpful to Tau in this regard, as Psy's spooks won't be going on the record. And as shocking as this is, I am a reliable source. I have never given information to a reporter that I knew was false. Providing good information to Tau for years has earned me points with his editor, who also has to sign off on my anonymity.

Journalism would die without anonymous sources. They take risks to leak stories that check the power of the rich and powerful. But the sword has two edges. Anonymous sourcing is used by the powerful to advance their agendas. It is incumbent on the news organization, the reporter, the editors, and their corporate counsel to determine the veracity of the information and the informant's motives. The majority of this responsibility falls on the reporter. While gathering information, they must understand how it fits into a broader agenda, should one exist. It almost always does.

Tau is a seasoned reporter who understands this game. I once pitched him some Psy-Group bullshit about Ukraine that he realized pretty fast was fake news. (It was literal fake news: Psy-Group was trying to manufacture something, and the version of the story that ultimately ran was a fake news broadcast.) Reporters don't just print whatever I want them to, unfortunately. Tau and I both understand the unspoken agreement: I have to dish everything, and misleading him will only cause my anonymity to evaporate.

"Okay," he says, taking a pen and notebook from his messenger bag. "Let's begin. I hope you brought your laptop."

Tau can't be the only reporter chasing after the Psy–Mueller connection. I need to cover my bases. I drop a line to a reporter from Bloomberg and start feeding him intel off the record. Every time I pitch this story, I'm gambling. Going all in. Every hand. It is a binary equation: I will either win or lose. And the result will be very, very public. There's no hiding a mistake on the front page of a newspaper.

PR operatives gamble every time we pitch a story. Sometimes we lose. Just like any good gambler, we try to minimize our losses. To do that, we must know what can go wrong. The editor could blow the headline. The paper could break the embargo date. It could misquote your client. It could accidentally quote you. An off-the-record statement could bleed into the story. Your adversary might have the goods on your client. A regulator or government might step in and skew the story. Other news might eclipse your story. The reporter you are working with might get scooped. Your source could get cold feet. And finally, it might turn out that your client has been lying to you the whole time.

You might think these things don't happen. They do. All of them have happened to me. We don't have room in this book for all the stories that have gone sideways in my career. Trust me, there are a lot.

Good PR operatives learn how to minimize the chance of damage. For a story to go my way, I need two things: time and information. In this instance, time is against me. I don't know which other reporters are on this story. They might be calling me soon. And I don't know if the Office of Special Counsel is going to leak my connection to the Psy-Group to the media. So I'll have to rely on information. I know which items resonate with which publications. Bloomberg eyes the money angle, so I reference the large transfers made through my bank account as being of great interest to the authorities.

The articles run in quick succession. Tau and his colleagues at the *Journal* publish in April, exposing Mueller's probe into foreign influence in Washington. The Bloomberg piece hits in May, naming the Psy-Group for the first time. My money angle works: "Mueller Asked About Money Flows to Israeli Social-Media Firm, Source Says," the headline reports. The *Wall Street Journal* follows up the next day with a piece on Psy-Group's partnership with Cambridge Analytica. I appear in the articles not as Phil Elwood, but as a person familiar with the work of Psy-Group.

My relief is short-lived. In May 2018, I get the call I've been dreading. It's from an investigative journalist with the *New York Times*. If there is one publication I'm afraid of in my situation, it's the *Times*. They are scooping everyone on Mueller.

"I'm writing a story on the connection between Psy-Group and Trump," the reporter says. "You're in it."

"Slow down," I say. "Can we meet?"

The reporter agrees to have a drink with me at Commissary. Right now, I'm the target. I need to turn myself into the source. "If my name is in your piece, my career is fucked," I say. I explain that I am a minor player in this story. I would be nothing more than collateral damage. And that if the *Times* names me, I will not be a source, and the paper's story may have factual errors. It's a Faustian deal with a twist. I am the devil this reporter knows.

"Okay," the reporter says. "Tell me everything you know."

I cough it all up. I tell the reporter how the Psy-Group works and the names of the major players. I hand over client lists. I let the *Times* reporter look through my laptop and forward documents from my email account. It's the most access I've ever granted a journalist, but I'm the most desperate I've ever been.

This is the wrong way to leak documents. I should have

taken a page from Daniel Ellsberg, the man responsible for one of the biggest leaks in U.S. government history. Sure, he got charged under the Espionage Act of 1917, but in the end he won a medal for it.

As a researcher with the RAND Corporation, Ellsberg had access to classified documents at the Pentagon. It was 1971. America was utterly disaffected by the conflict in Vietnam. The government was pushing the message that things were going just fine in Southeast Asia. Ellsberg knew the Pentagon's internal documents told another story. At a copy machine, he duplicated what he could. He then covertly met with members of Congress.

Ellsberg's strategy here was quite cunning: under the Speech and Debate Clause of the U.S. Constitution, no member of Congress can be prosecuted for what they say on the floor. That's right: a member of Congress could introduce the leaked information into the *Congressional Record*, making the whole thing public, and not face charges. This eventually happened, but congresspeople have never been known for having much of a spine. They need cover before acting.

Here comes the need for the Fourth Estate. Whistleblowers often use the press to give members of Congress cover—or "air support," as some practitioners call it. Ellsberg went to the *New York Times*. This was before email and Snapchat, so he leaked the Pentagon Papers the way it should be done today. If you are going to leak a document, do it in person. Print the thing off and physically hand it to a reporter. So many people leak documents via email. Email is forever. Once you hit Send, you have created what will some-day be a public document.

On June 13, 1971, the *New York Times* printed its first story on the leak. The government sued the paper. For fifteen days, the courts sorted out how the Constitution and the needs of the government should be balanced. During that time, Ellsberg went to the *Washington Post* while eluding an FBI manhunt. Two days prior to the Supreme Court's decision, Ellsberg outed himself as the source. The Court ruled in favor of the *New York Times*. Ellsberg was arrested and charged, but all charges against him were dismissed in May 1973.

That is how you leak a document. Stop emailing. Don't create a digital footprint. Go old-school, and do it in person. Otherwise, you will get caught. I'm being careless, using email, because my back is against the wall and I've already been caught by the FBI.

While I bite my nails waiting for the *New York Times* to publish, some more of my old sins come out of the past and into the press. The *Times*, Great Britain's oldest national daily newspaper, publishes an exclusive that reads, "Qatar Sabotaged 2022 World Cup Rivals with 'Black Ops': Whistleblower Reveals Ex-CIA Agents and PR Firm Were Hired in Dirty Tricks Campaign that Broke FIFA Rules." Somehow, the press is blaming all my activities relating to the Qatar bid on a retired CIA agent.

"I dodged a bullet," I tell Lindsay.

"You got lucky. Again," she says. "But when will this end?"

I have to stop this news cycle. Get the definitive piece written on the Psy-Group into a long-form publication.

Adam Entous agrees to meet me at Commissary. He's one of the best investigative journalists in the country and has the perfect background to do the definitive ten-thousand-word, no-one-will-ever-ask-questions-again treatise on Psy-Group in the *New Yorker*.

I drink mega mimosas while Entous sips water. I let him do keyword searches through my old emails to access Psy-Group documents. The Psy files have comically lax security; guessing the passwords is easy once you know the code names. When Entous types in "Mockingjay," he discovers that Psy-Group tried to influence a local hospital board election in Tulare, in California's San Joaquin Valley.

"They were so desperate to break into the American market that they were willing to rig a hospital board election," Entous says.

"They were willing to do a lot of things."

"They were basically bottom feeders," Entous says. "I'm picturing these ex-Mossad agents running around central California. This is a dark comedy."

Over the next few months, Entous and I exchange intel at Commissary. He travels to Israel to meet Royi Burstien. "He wanted to meet in a crowded place," says Entous when we debrief the trip. "He seemed quite nervous."

"Sounds like Royi," I say.

Entous is fascinated by Royi's career arc. "It starts with

good intentions: counterterrorism and security," he muses. "If Psy had stopped after Project Madison, they'd be heroes who infiltrated terrorist cells. But once they realize there's a broader market, it morphs, takes on a life of its own, because of the influence of money. And eventually that temptation lures you to do things that you're not that comfortable with, you know?"

"Yes, I know," I say, remembering my first days in PR, when I brought awareness to the war in Iraq by getting more people to see an antiwar documentary.

"It's not so different from your occupation."

"Not at all."

"In Psy's other operations, like the hospital board election, there's no reason for them to intervene except for money," Entous continues. "But sometimes you have to make these choices. We all make choices to support our families. We make compromises to get what we want. When I look at it from a human angle, I don't think they are such terrible people. Right?"

"Maybe," I say.

But this digs at a question in my head: Who is worse? The people I represent, doing things I know to be wrong? Or the person representing them? As a former student of ethics in undergraduate courses, I am not sure where Kant would come down on my question. But I know who the worst human is.

The *New York Times* story runs on October 8, 2018. The headline reads, "Rick Gates Sought Online Manipulation

Plans from Israeli Intelligence Firm for Trump Campaign."
I read all 1,800 words while holding my breath. My name
doesn't appear. I learn that Psy-Group is now in liquidation.

"I feel like I can breathe," I say.

"I wouldn't go that far," Lindsay says. "But it's a win. We'll
take it. By the way, I transferred you money for this month."

"Sorry."

"You'll pay it back," she says. "You'll figure something out
soon."

Lindsay has been giving me an allowance. Keeping your
name out of the press doesn't put food on the table. She's
had to start cutting costs to account for our being a single-
income household. Every time Lindsay's money hits my
account, I feel like a deadbeat. I'm meant to be a partner,
not a dependent. My father, a minister, always said we make
our own heavens and hells here on earth. My world is looking more and more like a hellish Hieronymus Bosch painting
every day. This time, it's one I painted with my own hand.

"Let's get out of DC this weekend," Lindsay suggests. "It's
been a lot. Let's go hide out."

"Sounds nice."

"But you've got to shower before we get in the car," she
says.

We head out to the Eastern Shore. During the drive, as
we pass over the Chesapeake Bay, my mind manufactures
the idea that Lindsay is going to leave me. I'm damaged.
A PR guy who can't work in PR. By the time we pull up to
our little house, I've convinced myself I've already lost her.

When I think about what life will look like after she's gone, I see nothing but black, empty space. How do I begin to ask for forgiveness for being so reckless? So selfish?

I've spent my whole life creating narratives. In PR, a good narrative has a beginning, middle, and end. Truly effective narratives become invasive thoughts we plant in the public's mind. The machinery of PR twists truth to whichever way we want the wind to blow. It's the same game Royi Burstien played: influence how people think by putting your ideas into their heads. Suicidal ideation works the same way. My disordered mind constructs a narrative with a beginning, middle, and end. The beginning is the idea that I need to end my own life. The middle is planning how to do it. The end is the execution. And like the best narratives I've created in PR, this idea is invasive. It changes the way I think. And it won't leave me alone.

We need lightbulbs for the back porch. I drive to a little hardware store full of items you use to build a life. A young couple inquires about the price of new grill for their back patio. They are giddy, swept up in plans for next summer. I drift up and down the aisles, examining hammers and saws. A length of rope calls to me. I could loop it around the stairs leading to the attic. I read labels on yellow bags of rodent poison: "Guaranteed to Kill." One aisle over, a clerk stacks bottles of bleach and cleaning products mothers warn their children never to drink. The thought of poison bubbling in my stomach brings on an acute panic attack. My throat nearly closes up before I can swallow a Xanax. I relax and wonder if Xanax is lethal. My phone tells me yes, especially if you mix it with alcohol.

"Where are the lightbulbs?" Lindsay inquires when I return home empty-handed.

Back in DC, I stop taking Xanax. Not because the dark feeling is gone, but because I've decided to start saving the pills up. I stockpile thirty and run the empty bottle through the washing machine, set to "Hot." At the pharmacy, I show the warped plastic to a woman in a white coat and tell her the pills have been ruined. She hands over another sixty.

The next Friday morning, I bring Lindsay coffee as she gets ready for work. "I'm going to take the car out to the shore today," I say. "Work on my résumé."

"Sounds like a plan," she answers, her mind preoccupied with end-of-week deadlines. She will be busy with the Ladies' Lounge all weekend.

"I love you," I call when she's halfway out the door. "See you soon."

"Lahvya!" I hear her disembodied voice shout.

When I grab the car keys, Darth Vader hides under the bed. I try to get his attention, but he won't come to me. I just want to say goodbye.

I cry twice on the drive out to Maryland.

First when I reach the city limits of DC, the place where I've lived my entire adult life. Most people are taught from a very young age to hate Washington. It's the focal point for Americans' distrust in their government. But it doesn't have to be that way. After twenty years in this city, I have met so many people who want to make the world a better place. Idealism drives so much of this town. It gives it life and a character far removed from the popular imagination. I'm crying because I can't say I ever had that character. I'm mourning an idealism that I only ever truly held with a sense of envy, not conviction.

I cry again when I cross the Bay Bridge. In my rearview mirror, I see the sun is setting over the bay, but I'm not moved by the beauty of the fall light on the horizon. It's the dark water below that stirs my chest. When I think about what's next, what happens after, my mind can only conjure that endless, empty water.

I pull into town just after sunset. At Al's Pizza, I talk to Al. I've gotten him hooked on Jeffrey Archer novels. He's just finished *As the Crow Flies*, which chronicles the life of a fruit seller who built an empire only to have it taken from him in the end. "In the last scene of the book, he's back hawking fruit and vegetables," Al says. "He ends up right where he started."

After a few beers at Al's, I go to our house and do some writing of my own. A note titled "For Lindsay." I add pages until I fall asleep on the couch. The next evening, I smoke a joint and look at the stars in the country sky. Turkey vultures, bigger than eagles, perch on our roof. I go to my favorite restaurant in town and have a steak with a good bottle of red wine. I chew the steak slowly and drink the wine fast.

After dinner, I sit on the couch, open my laptop, and delete every file except the one titled "For Lindsay." I write my password on a Post-it note and stick it to the screen. Then I put on a movie. I don't remember which one, but I know it's not *Star Wars*. I take a Xanax, then a few more, and then pour the rest of the pills into a pile on the coffee table. The film begins to shimmer, then blur. I close my eyes and picture the earth just before skydiving out of an airplane. See how it curves. See the ground that will rush up to meet me. All that's left to do is fall.

CHAPTER 11

Deadline

Lindsay pulls into the drive-through of a Dunkin' Donuts on U.S. Route 301, near the shores of the Chesapeake Bay. She orders two large coffees and a box of Munchkins. She hands me my cup and turns up the radio. We get back on the highway, sitting mute as mile markers drag by outside the window. Lindsay is quiet only in times of turmoil, a remnant of her midwestern upbringing. At funerals back home, everyone stares straight ahead so they can't see who is crying.

I sip my coffee. Caffeine cuts a small river of energy through the aching in my skull. Another fear hangover. This time, I'm not afraid of the Doctor or of my name ending up in a *New York Times* exposé. I'm scared of myself. Of how close I came to ending my life last night.

Just after sunset, I was preparing to swallow a handful of Xanax when a call came through from my friend and college debate partner Rachel Sullivan. For some reason, I put down the pills and picked up the phone. Talking to Rachel was like being back in a debate round. She stayed level and rational while I told her I wanted to end my life. She had a plan. Options. A way out. That's what we are taught as debaters. How to solve problems. Rachel took on the role of Scheherazade, the narrator of *One Thousand and One Nights*, who tells stories to keep a king from cutting off her head. Instead of telling me a story to spare her own life, Rachel kept an argument going that saved mine. She was on and off the phone with me for hours, and in between calls, she got hold of Lindsay. Rachel told her to find a way to get to me. And not to wait a second.

When Lindsay flashed through the door, she threw her arms around me. She read my suicide note once. Then we deleted it together. Next, she went after the pills. She took the ones in front of me and went through my bag to make sure she got them all. I still don't know what she did with them. She held me like a kid with a skinned knee, and I cried until I was steady enough to get into bed.

As we get closer to DC, I watch Lindsay drive, her eyes wide and focused on the road ahead. She's always been the strong one, solving the problems I can't stop creating. I'm still terrified of losing her. And I'm scared of how difficult it will be to get better.

It's still morning when we reach home. Lindsay calls in sick to work and schedules an emergency session with Dr. Hellmann, my therapist. Lindsay guides me toward the car, watching closely in case I decide to bolt for Commissary.

"I'm going to sit in with you, Phil," she tells me when we pull up to the doctor's office. "Whatever drove you to this point, we need to talk through it together, and I want to make sure you tell the doctor all of it."

I mumble my agreement.

I tell Dr. Hellmann the whole story. How the fear I've felt for years has built up into a tunnel of darkness and how, after the Psy-Group fiasco, I didn't see a way out. I made a plan—which doctors who study suicide know makes you much more likely to go through with it. Dr. Hellmann tells me more about bipolar II disorder. I ride massive highs—like the insane rush I got from masterminding a trade war between Antigua and the United States. But I need to learn how to withstand the lows, which feel like long valleys of despair.

"I didn't know you'd been thinking about this for so long," Lindsay says.

Dr. Hellmann wants to see me twice a week for the next two months. In one of our sessions, I vent that my former client Bashar al-Assad has been in the news for killing a child with a chlorine gas attack. She listens and then holds up a finger.

"I'm hearing a lot of shame," she says. "And maybe rightfully so. But can you tell me about an assignment you're proud of?"

"Define 'proud.'"

"*You* define it for me."

"Do you remember the *Simpsons* episode where Homer becomes an astronaut?" I ask.

"No, but go on."

"Well, Bart says, 'Wow, my dad an astronaut. I feel so full of . . . what's the opposite of shame?' Marge asks if he means 'pride.' He says, 'No, not that far from shame.' Homer asks, 'Less shame?' And Bart smiles. I've got a story that makes me feel like that."

I tell Dr. Hellmann that in 2016, *BuzzFeed News*'s Daniel Wagner asked if I knew anything about Donald Trump's dealings with Muammar Gaddafi. Peter Brown often told me that Trump cozied up to the dictator because he wanted access to the Libyan Investment Authority, a sixty-billion-dollar pool of money. Why else would Trump let the most hated man in the tristate area pitch a tent on his lawn? A BLJ employee (who happened to be Martha Stewart's nephew) once told me that, post-tent, Trump wanted to meet with Gaddafi to discuss business opportunities.

As an anonymous source, I filled in *BuzzFeed*'s team on the golf games I helped set up in Florida for the Libyan ambassador, and on how Trump tried to gain access to Libya's sovereign wealth fund. I showed them emails, a signed document from a Trump intermediary, and other correspondence, and I introduced Dan Wagner to a BLJ staffer whom he convinced to go on the record. The resulting piece, "The Donald and the Dictator," was a damning portrait of Trump's overtures to the Libyan regime. In the first presidential debate, Hillary Clinton hit Trump on Gaddafi, claiming the two did business together. The article must have been in her debate prep.

"Why don't you feel unqualified pride about that?" Dr. Hellmann asks. "You helped hold power accountable."

"Because I really wish I got paid for it," I reply.

"We'll talk about that next time," she says.

An Uber deposits me at my second mental health appointment of the afternoon. Over the last five years, Dr. Agarwal has cycled me through fifteen different cocktails of antidepressants, antipsychotics, and mood stabilizers. Today I'm on four medications. Some pills can't be taken during daylight hours. Others I can't take after dark. I feel like a Gremlin, and Lindsay calls me Gizmo when she sees me gobbling pills at odd hours.

"How are the medications working?" Dr. Agarwal asks.

"Some bad," I say. "Some worse."

"I think you suffer from treatment-resistant depression," she says, adding another diagnosis to the pile.

"After what I've just gone through, that sounds like a death sentence," I say.

"There's one other thing we can try," Dr. Agarwal says. "Ketamine therapy. It's known as the treatment of last resort. Think about it."

That evening when I come home, Lindsay asks, "So, are you all fixed yet?"

"Yup," I reply. "All better."

It's been our running joke for years, but I know I've put

Lindsay through the wringer. Now that Chester Creek is kaput, and my legal bills have burned through the twenty-five thousand dollars I put into savings, I need a steady job for her sake and mine. An FBI agent I met during an investigation talks to me about consulting for the Bureau on how to deal with the press during hostage situations. I'm thrilled by the chance to do something useful with my skill set, something finally aboveboard.

"I have to warn you," I tell the agent. "My file with your organization is pretty substantial."

Because I've been investigated by the very agency I hope will employ me, and because I've worked as a foreign agent, I can't pass a security clearance check. Some doors are forever closed to a guy like me, which is probably for the best. I'm still radioactive in Washington's respectable circles, so I must return to the world I know. I've been in the PR machine since I was twenty-four years old. I don't know how to do anything else.

The beginning of a new day makes the Acela train's windows glow like the heated glass of oven doors. It's just after sunrise, and the business-class cabin is filled with people typing on laptops. People headed to work. For the first time in nearly a year, so am I.

The first task my new boss wants me to perform is to prevent a hit job on the firm itself. When the firm is the story, you know you've got a problem. And this place has a problem. I'm there to stop it. I know the reporter who is coming after them. He's won awards. He's put people in jail. He's a killer. I tell my boss it's not a fight we can win, and I propose another tactic.

Detonating the bomb in a safe location is a PR trick of last resort. If you know you are about to be punched in the face, would you rather have Mike Tyson do it or some guy named "Mike" from the accounting department? I'd take my chances with the guy who is good with spreadsheets. In this analogy, the champ would be the *New York Times*, and Mike from accounting would be email newsletters, less prominent digital news organizations, and trade and local publications. Outlets like this are often referred to as "tier-two" publications. There are great reporters at these publications, and they often break news that forces the "tier-one" publications to play catch-up. However, unless it is a really big story, breaking news in a tier-two will ensure that it is not covered in the larger publications. This makes the tier-twos a relatively safe location.

If you catch wind that one of the tier-one publications— the *New York Times*, the *Washington Post*, the *Wall Street Journal*—or one of the wire services is investigating your client, you need to do damage assessment. Find out exactly what they have on the client. Force the client to tell you the truth. Then ask your client who they would like to get hit by? Tyson or the geek from accounting? This usually clarifies their thinking. You then pitch the negative story yourself. You compile all the data and resources needed to publish it.

Leave nothing out. No room for additional reporting. Then give the reporter an hours-long embargo date. Tell them you are going to other reporters in a few hours. This is to ensure that you "scoop" the tier-one publication already pursuing your client.

The "tier-two" story runs. If you have been in touch with a reporter for the *New York Times* in this hypothetical example, they will call you. And they will be apoplectic. Your relationship with this reporter is now over.

This is not the most sustainable media strategy. You cannot do this on a regular basis. However, once in a while—after you've weighed the story's importance against creating an enemy out of a journalist—it's worth it.

It's not good enough for my new boss, though. She wants a hit job on the guy doing a hit job. It's an impossible task.

Her next request of me escalates things. It involves spies, hacked data, and a notoriously dangerous foreign embassy. I'm supposed to be the fixer, making the connections so that the information and money can change hands. My boss assures me it's legal and that if I'm successful my firm will get millions of dollars. And I'll get another helping of PTSD, maybe another visit from the FBI.

I have the demoralizing realization that I'm caught in a loop. I'm trapped in the bowels of a PR machine where I spin around and around questionable operatives, shady deals, and legal peril. The faces change. The offices change. My job remains the same. I grease the wheels of a machine that pulls the levers for those in power, or simply those who have money, to keep those same people in power. And I'm good at it.

Part of me wants to break this loop. Walk out on this job right now and open a bar in Maryland. I'd man the kitchen and tell war stories to the regulars. But my instinct, the part of me that has pulled this off for nearly two decades, thinks, *You know how to do this. This is all you know and all you will ever know. This is who you are. Now go do what you do.*

At BLJ, I would have gone through with this assignment without thinking twice. After my suicide attempt, a switch in my brain has finally been flipped. I can't start heading down a road that will only lead back to that dark place, because the next time, I won't crawl back out. So, I stop, sit Lindsay down at the dining room table, and tell her what I'm about to do.

"Are you out of your fucking mind?" she asks. "The FBI was *just here.*"

"Maybe they'll get the right apartment this time," I say, trying to break bad news with humor, something my shrink says I do a little too often.

"This sounds like it's breaking so many laws, I don't know where to start. You need to start by calling your lawyer."

"I haven't done anything yet," I say.

"It's your choice," Lindsay says, anger leaving her face, replaced by a frightening look of resignation. "It's insane to me that you'd even consider it, but you need to take care of yourself. You can't trust your firm to protect you. Their interest is in making money. It's your choice, Phil. It's always your choice. Just be prepared to live with the consequences."

I head up to the roof and call my lawyer.

"As usual, Lindsay is right," Saltzman says. "This is all kinds of illegal."

I'm in Sonoma, California, attending a swanky wedding for one of Lindsay's old colleagues at a liberal think tank. At the reception, guests in eco-friendly, sustainably sourced cotton attire sip champagne at a winery surrounded by ornate gardens. It's a DC cocktail party moved three thousand miles west. With more linen.

I'm standing with a group of Hillary Clinton acolytes when my phone rings. I step away and take the call. My boss harangues me about PowerPoint slides for one of our questionable clients. If anyone at the wedding heard this conversation, I'd be asked to leave.

"I can't get to my computer right now," I say. "I told you I was away this weekend."

"Do it," comes the curt reply.

I step into a hedge garden and call Richard Levick, who listens while I vent in a whisper. "I can't do this anymore," I say. "Everyone at this wedding is a decent human being who thinks they're saving the world, and I'm the guy on the other side."

"It's just client work," Levick consoles. "It's like when we repped the payday lenders."

These calls are a PR guy's version of a support group. I can talk with another flak without fear of judgment, knowing they won't bat an eyelash at things that would make the policy institute set at this reception throw a drink in my face. Levick understands because he's done these things, too.

"It's not as bad as Nigeria," he tells me. "Come see me when you're back."

When I land in DC, I grab a cab directly to the stone house Levick lives in at the edge of Rock Creek Park. It's stabilizing to see my old mentor. He's just come back from a hike in the park, and he's wearing a gray tracksuit. In his study, he uncorks the expensive stuff, and I tell him about the dangerous assignment I refused, the one involving a foreign embassy. It's difficult to shock a man who's been in the PR game for three decades, but Levick is incensed.

"I'm not a practicing lawyer. But I'm enough of a lawyer to know that you need to get away from this firm," he tells me.

"What do I do?"

"Quit."

"I need the job," I say.

"'An older boy told me to do it' is not a legal defense," Levick says. "You are going to be held responsible for any actions you take."

It's good advice.

The next morning, I head to the office. I think of Levick's words from last night and call Lindsay. I've finally set a deadline for myself, which means something different to me than it does to journalists. The word *deadline* originated in the American Civil War, when a line was drawn in the dirt around prisons. Guards were instructed to shoot any prisoner who crossed the line—the "deadline." I've drawn my own deadline in the sand, knowing that if I cross it, I won't come back. I'd like to say that a moral epiphany or a newfound ethical backbone spurred this decision. Truth is, it's pragmatic. I set this deadline to stay alive.

"I think I need to quit," I tell Lindsay.

"Do it," she says. "Just go. You'll find something better."

"Thank you," I say, floored by her confidence in me.

I am barely off the phone with Lindsay when I call human resources. "My time here has come to an end," I say.

"When do you want your last day to be?"

"Right now."

"The CEO is in town and would like to talk to you."

"I don't think I'd learn very much from that conversation."

I grab my things and beeline for the exit. I'm almost out the door when I see a junior staffer looking at me. "Where are you going?" he asks. "We have a meeting in ten."

"I just quit."

"You can do that?" he asks.

CHAPTER 12

Fix You

A steady-handed nurse locates a vein in my arm and slips in a butterfly needle. I plug in my earphones as she attaches a syringe of ketamine mixed with saline solution to an infusion pump. She pushes a button on the pump, and the pump begins to depress the syringe millimeter by millimeter. I sit back in the movie theater–style chair, start my playlist, and wait for the drug to hit my bloodstream.

The first wave is subtle, a warm chemical wash. Then it builds, and I dissociate from my body. The Pink Floyd song in my ears is my only tether to physical reality. Distortions appear—first circles made of color and light, then a parade of images. I flash to memories, viewing them from the perspective of a dispassionate observer. Moments from a life that belongs to someone else.

A young man with raccoon circles under his eyes sits outside a familiar bar. He scribbles a jumble of words about the

World Cup on a cocktail napkin. He slumps, his body tense with worry. People inside the bar laugh and shout jovially. The young man is alone with his drink and his task. The cocktail napkin morphs into a newspaper. Then a smartphone, its screen covered with texts and notifications. The young man does not yet know about Qatar's neo-feudalist Kafala labor system. He is unaware that Bangladeshi, Indian, Nepalese, and Filipino migrant workers will slave to build gleaming, monstrous soccer stadiums. He does not know that thousands of these indentured servants will die before the first match is played. I watch the young man, understanding that he is but a small part of a larger machine. I hold him accountable for his many mistakes, but I do not hate him for them.

Coldplay's "Fix You" begins playing in my earphones, guiding me to a memory of Lindsay's touch the night I nearly ended my life. I understand how badly she wanted to help me overcome my depression, feel the force of her love as she rushed to my rescue in my moment of greatest need. I become more aware of how lucky I am to have her support. I feel connected to my wife in ways I cannot express but am deeply grateful to experience.

After forty-five minutes, I feel myself return to the room. Dr. Patrick Oliver, a stocky, middle-aged man in a white lab coat, comes to check on me.

"How was the strength of the dose?" he asks.

"Perfect," I say.

Dr. Oliver has devoted his life to helping people with

suicidal ideation, yet he speeds through the streets of DC on a Ducati racing motorcycle. We get along just fine. When I walked into the MindPeace Clinic a year and a half ago, Dr. Oliver asked what had brought me in.

"Several things fucked me up," I said. "My job being one of them."

Dr. Oliver explained that my brain is powered by neural pathways that look like branches of a tree; they are delicate and sophisticated. Decades of mistreated mental illness and PTSD incurred from my job have killed those branches. Ketamine helps regrow them. Without it, depression creates a delta between how I should feel and how I actually feel. If the events of the day make a healthy brain feel nine out of ten on a happiness scale, they make my brain register a two.

I'm not alone, especially in DC. Many of Dr. Oliver's patients have high-level security clearances. They work on the Hill and at the Pentagon. Dr. Oliver has a hypothesis that high-stress jobs burn out neural pathways at an alarming rate, and though this hypothesis hasn't been scientifically proven it certainly mirrors my experience.

My case is laced with an extra tinge of irony. The very essence of my job requires that I communicate effectively, yet I struggle to do that in my own mind. The very thing I'm so effective at professionally, my brain is incapable of on a physiological level.

Ketamine isn't a magic bullet, but I've felt steady improvement over the last year and a half. I feel like my disease is being treated for the first time ever. Plus it's a legal way to get really high for an hour every few weeks. Lindsay says I'm no longer as flat, that I'm more communicative and emotive, and that I laugh like I used to.

And ever since Dr. Oliver put a needle in my arm, I haven't been drawn to work that smells illegal or worked for any blood-soaked dictators. I've got my deadline, and I'm sticking to it. Like Doc Brown in *Back to the Future*, I've survived stealing from the Libyans, and I want to do something meaningful with my second chance.

Surprisingly, the opportunity comes through Preston. He video-calls me from his home trading desk, sipping an IPA drafted fresh from the kegerator hardwired into the granite wet bar he had installed last spring.

"I'm plugged in with a group of former special forces operators and contractors," he says.

"Doesn't surprise me."

"One of them, a guy named RJ, owns a company that makes precision weapons for special forces outfits," Preston says. "When tier-one outfits need mission-specific one-off gear, RJ provides it. He designed and built my daughter's rifle by hand using a micrometer. It took ten months. He makes art."

"I'll bet you two hit it off."

"On the East Coast, we're functionally behind enemy lines for anything concerning the Second Amendment," Preston says. "Guys with a common interest in weaponry can smell each other like animals."

"Same breed."

"Bingo," Preston says. "RJ is working with a team of former tier-one operators who are running ratlines with active special forces on the ground in Ukraine. These guys are under deep cover observing and reporting on the Russian invasion."

RJ's team has discovered that Putin's war has put the Ukrainian Junior Olympic gymnastics team in grave danger. In the former Eastern Bloc, gymnasts are as popular as baseball players are in the United States—which makes them prime Russian targets. The gymnasts are all under the age of seventeen and scattered around the country. But RJ's team has come up with an extraction plan. Charter a passenger plane into an active war zone and transport the athletes to the U.S. Olympic training center in Colorado Springs.

"I can secure the airplane," Preston says. "I hate to say it, but we need your contacts in DC. Can you grease some wheels?"

Over the next two months, I set up Zoom calls between RJ and the media, who want an exclusive, and connect RJ with potential donors who can fund the extraction. The rescue op stalls when we hit State Department red tape. Transporting minors over international borders may trip human trafficking laws. Undeterred, a member of RJ's team liaisons with a volunteer firm of retired special forces operators called Project SIRIN. Project SIRIN's network gathers intel on supplies the Ukrainian military needs in the combat theater. The Ukrainians desperately require night vision and thermal optics, which are used to detect an enemy in darkness through heat. As they defend their cities from Russian attack, the Ukrainians have no nighttime capabilities. Sitting ducks in the dark.

"Thermal optics are god powers," Preston informs me on the three-way Zoom with RJ.

"They'll give the tip of the spear the ability to assault at night, when the Russians are sleeping," RJ says.

"I don't care if you're in a ghillie suit, you show up bright as a set of headlights in the middle of a field," Preston adds. "It's a kill cheat code. I have thermals mounted on my forward optic on what I call my medium-sized gun."

I wonder what Preston has equipped on his large-size gun.

"You can't really appreciate thermals until you use them," Preston continues.

"Hope I never have to," I say.

"I'll take a bad firearm with a good optic over a good firearm with a bad optic any day of the week."

Project SIRIN can facilitate the transfer of night vision and thermal optics to Ukrainian snipers. Delivery requires navigating a web of operators and regulators. Any transfer of arms technology, down to a ballistics calculator, must abide by International Traffic in Arms Regulations (ITAR). If civilians like us shipped military-grade materials without ITAR approval, we'd go to federal prison, likely for the rest of our lives.

But I happen to drink with an arms dealer at Commissary. If you want to legally move guns, money, or people around the earth, she knows how to do the paperwork. Soon, the optics are loaded onto a cargo plane bound for a secret destination. In Ukraine, the matériel has an immediate impact. RJ's team receives dispatches from Ukrainian special forces thanking them for the resources to defend their homeland. "They are not only pushing back the Russians, they are going on counteroffensives," RJ says, filling me in. "They are taking back their cities."

The American operators in Ukraine call the operation one of the most incredible moments in their twenty-plus years working with local forces. The motto stitched onto their jackets reads, "De oppresso liber," Latin for "Free the Oppressed." Helping underarmed, outgunned Ukrainians fight against Putin's tyrannical invasion fulfills their ultimate call to service.

But the war isn't over. Russia mounts counteroffensives. Publicizing Project SIRIN's work will drive more funding for aid. I know that Karoun Demirjian, a national security reporter with the *Washington Post*, will be interested in the story.

"This is new," Demirjian says when I call. "Aren't you the guy who used to work for dictators?"

"Yes," I say. "Yes, I am."

If there is a silver lining to having worked for the likes of Gaddafi and Assad, it's that reporters will always take my call. They know I'm usually mixed up in something interesting.

At the MindPeace Clinic, a nurse hands me an iPad. I scroll through a series of multiple-choice questions, each with four potential answers that feed data to my "Mood Monitor."

Feeling down, depressed, or hopeless?
B. *Several days.*

Feeling bad about yourself or that you are a failure or have let yourself or your family down?
B. *Several days.*

Thoughts that you would be better off dead or thoughts of hurting yourself in some way?
D. *Not at all.*

The final question is weighted more heavily than all the others. I've selected "Not at all" for the last two years. My iPhone's Mood Monitor registers "Moderate"—safely in the "yellow" zone. If my mood dips into "Severe," the red zone, it's time to take action. Schedule an extra infusion or a session with Dr. Hellmann. Talk to Lindsay. The same way I take Lipitor for my high cholesterol.

Dr. Oliver comes into the infusion room holding a syringe filled with 160mg of ketamine. "What exactly does your job entail?" he asks, squirting the ketamine into a larger syringe full of saline solution.

"I work in a very disturbing kind of public relations," I say. "I help people with serious reputational problems."

"You know," Dr. Oliver says, "ketamine has a reputational problem."

"People think we snort it off a coffee table."

"The term *k-hole* has done untold damage to my practice," Dr. Oliver says.

"Maybe I can help with that."

"Let's talk after your infusion," he says and then rockets me to another dimension.

After I've returned to my body and waited out the requisite fifteen minutes, during which a nurse makes sure my blood pressure has stabilized, Dr. Oliver comes back into the infusion room. As the nurse slips out the needle and places a Band-Aid over the injection site, Dr. Oliver gives me a quick history lesson.

Ketamine was introduced in the 1960s and later used as a battlefield anesthetic in the Vietnam War. It works fast. The World Health Organization lists it as one of our essential medicines. It's also been a club drug known as Special K for the last fifty years. The popular imagination and countless Instagram memes think it's a "horse tranquilizer" because it's also used in veterinary medicine. This stigma makes patients unwilling to try ketamine therapy.

Dr. Oliver wants to rebrand the drug by emphasizing its efficacy for suicidal ideation. When he was an emergency room doctor, one his patients killed herself, and Dr. Oliver devoted the rest of his career to suicide prevention. And he began by researching alternative interventions. He thinks the way to fight the narrative that ketamine is a club drug prone to abuse is to show it as a lifesaving treatment. I couldn't agree more, since it saved my life. Changing the narrative on something as misunderstood as ketamine takes something as drastic as suicide.

It's tough to get press hits for suicide stories. Doesn't make for good morning TV. People change the channel.

Americans really don't like talking about mental health problems. In this country, one person kills themselves every eleven minutes. Forty-eight thousand people in 2021. Not talking about it really isn't working.

I wear my mental health on my sleeve—I've told FBI agents about my ketamine treatment. They think it's fascinating. For the press, I need an inroad to inject ketamine into the suicide debate. Dr. Oliver has just concluded a yearlong study that might do just that. It is one I myself participated in by answering questions on that iPad every week. After studying more than four hundred patients, Dr. Oliver's team observed that after ten infusions of ketamine, 72 percent of study participants saw improvement in their mood; 38 percent were symptom-free. Most critically, fifteen infusions decreased suicidal ideation by at least 85 percent.

I suggest taking the story to health reporter Meryl Kornfield at the *Washington Post*. I send Kornfield a draft of the study, soon to be published in the *Journal of Clinical Psychiatry*. Kornfield interviews Oliver and MindPeace Clinic patients. Her headline: "Nothing Seemed to Treat Their Depression. Then They Tried Ketamine." It might as well be talking about me.

"For years, Jason Anthony wondered why anyone would sing along to music alone in their car, an act of indulgence," Kornfield writes.

Throughout his 15-year battle with depression, Anthony, 52, could barely get out of bed. He kept empty liter-size soda bottles nearby for when he couldn't get to the bathroom. Showering and walking out the front door was a feat. He wouldn't have thought to amuse himself with a tune. But after working out at his home gym on a recent July weekend, Anthony, a criminal defense attorney in Richmond, found himself serenading his three yellow labradors [*sic*] with 1980s hair band tunes. And it wasn't an act. Anthony joked about the impromptu show as a nurse at MindPeace Clinic in Richmond prepared the treatment he credited with his newfound mental well-being: ketamine.

I finally have an answer to my therapist's question "Can you tell me about an assignment you're proud of?"

The next time I call the MindPeace Clinic, I get a busy signal. After two more tries, I get through to a receptionist, who says they can't fit me in for two weeks.

"Ever since that article, we've been booked solid," he says.

"I'm the reason you're booked up," I say. "Can you fit me in?"

They do, and when I arrive, Dr. Oliver is thrilled to see me. "New patients have been calling the clinic all week," he says.

"Do I get a kickback?" I joke.

"Four of them were suicidal," Dr. Oliver says. "That article saved lives."

* * *

After today's infusion, I order an Uber. On the ride back to Logan Circle, the effects of the drug linger, placing me in a reflective state. My thoughts run in smooth lines that generate perspective.

All the worst impulses my brain sends down my spinal cord have been tempered by ketamine therapy. Those dark impulses still lurk in the part of my frontal lobe that governs impulse control, but I can intercept them before they turn into action. For twenty years, I've done whatever a story required, risking my life and my freedom. Even when my life was in danger, I took wild chances for my clients. All for a few thousand headlines.

All the worst parts of my mind make me a great PR guy. I've been told by employers, reporters, and clients that I'm one of the most dangerous people in the business. I'm proud of my work, but I'm not proud of what I've done. I've manipulated narratives—even invented them when needed—to fix problems for a client. My stories didn't occur in a vacuum. They circulated out into the world. And they changed it. Sometimes for the worse. *Often* for the worse. I helped Qatar win the World Cup bid, one of my deepest regrets. I'm not proud to say I've seen the destruction my handiwork has created. We live in dangerous times, and my industry helped make them so.

All the worst places in the world have always had a business-class ticket with my name on it. I've always been in the wrong place at the right time. I flacked for Gaddafi and Assad in the halcyon days of the Arab Spring. I fell in with Israeli spies just before the Mueller investigation. I met Kim Dotcom six weeks before his arrest. I've been there when a government has collapsed, present when the subpoenas came down. You may say: *Isn't that the* wrong *time?* I'd say: it's when history happens. Lindsay calls me "the Forrest Gump of DC" because I've been behind the scenes of so many global events and historical moments you've read about in the news. My wife may be right: stupid is as stupid does. But at least I've gotten a front-row seat.

All the worst humans taught me that money is everything and nothing. Peter Brown's maxim "Anything is possible with the right amount of money" is true. The world proves him right again and again. The United States is the only democracy in the history of humanity that believes *as a matter of law* that money is speech. The Supreme Court created this precedent with the *Buckley v. Valeo* decision in 1976 and cemented it with *Citizens United* in 2010, giving all the worst humans all the worst tools.

But so many of my clients have had all the money in the world and have still been petty, vindictive, and perpetually unsatisfied. I've never met anyone as joyless as Mutassim Gaddafi. And I didn't make as much money as you'd imagine in the PR machine. It didn't make me a rich man.

But I never did it for the money. I did it for the story.

All the worst humans taught me what power really means. I've never felt like a powerful person, but I've wielded a lot of power. I'm an operative who flips a switch; the person actually in charge is the one who owns the machine. Elon Musk *wields* power; his Saudi financial backers *have* power. You may believe that Musk is currently the richest person in the world, but if the Kingdom of Saudi Arabia disapproved of his actions, they could collapse his empire with a few well-executed trades. In my case, I was able to wield the power of the press to shame Saudi Arabia into releasing a Turkish barber, but the power to save his life came from my client's instructions. There is always another man behind another curtain.

All the worst humans have given me a complicated relationship with the truth. They have often asked me to lie to reporters, but I've told only one bald-faced lie in my career (that I can remember). Don't believe me if you want to, but it's true. I've learned not to lie because so many awful people have asked me to do so. But I don't tell the truth, strictly speaking. My job requires me to tell the truth over a period of time. I tell *parts* of the truth at each step of the process. "You just tell them what you did right, and you leave out the rest!" as Nicolas Cage says in a wonderfully terrible movie called *Snake Eyes*. I hold many journalists in such high esteem because I envy their uncomplicated relationship to the truth. Journalism, like science, should be the quest for truth. It's because of the respect I have for journalists that I will not lie to them. But I've dreamed up some exceptionally creative pitches.

All the worst ideas led to all the best stories.

All the best stories—stories that have deposed rulers;

sent people to jail; freed people from jail; crashed public companies; brought together the world's human rights activists, and been protested by many of those same activists; glamorized villains; punished thieves; influenced economies; and pushed nations to the brink of financial collapse—they all started with a phone call. Your phone rings, and the first draft of history is on the other end.

And you have to pick up. You always pick up. Because if you don't, you don't get a say in writing that draft of history. You're just another guy sitting in an Uber watching the world go by outside the window.

If you pick up the phone, everything changes. You enter a liminal space where truth and reality can be whatever you want. It's almost as if the world freezes, and if you're good at what you do in PR, you can manipulate things—people, facts, the truth—before the world starts back up again. It doesn't matter what the truth is. The facts get changed, the public takes up your narrative, and you watch as the world resumes turning.

But you have to pick up the phone.

My phone is ringing now, as the car passes the Lincoln Memorial. When I look at the name on the screen, I get a hot, vibrating feeling, the feeling I've chased for twenty years, the feeling that's like jumping out of an airplane. It's Richard Levick. I may have left his firm years ago, but we have never really stopped working together.

As usual, Levick lays out his agenda up front. "Phil, I have two items we need to discuss," he says. "One is personal. One is work-related. Number one: I have cancer. Number two: I need you for a job."

"Hold on," I say. "Let's go back to number one."

"I'm going to beat it. My doctors give me an eighty-five percent chance of survival," he says. "Can we move on to the work-related matter?"

"Fine," I say, knowing I'll have to pry further details out of his junior agents.

"We have a new client," he continues. "This project will be on the front page of every newspaper around the world."

A warm sensation washes over me.

"And I need you," Levick says. "They have enough resources to put you on staff full time. This time, we'll be on the side of the good guys. But we'll need every dirty trick you have."

When Levick tells me the name of the client, I'm hit by the rush of an idea. Maybe it's the last of the ketamine in my system, but when I begin gaming out the strategy, the hot, flat streets outside the car window seem suspended in time and then disappear completely, and I'm no longer sitting in the back of an Uber.

I'm back on an airplane over Antigua, on my way to pitch a prime minister.

I'm back in the Abuja Hilton trying to run a game on Malala.

I'm floating in a beautiful darkness pulling the strings.

The next afternoon, I take the elevator up to the rooftop of my apartment. I do my best thinking up here, where I can see all of DC in all its squat, swampy glory. To the south is the dome of the Capitol Building, where I first rubbed elbows with the masters of this universe when I was twenty. And there's the Jefferson Memorial, where I proposed to Lindsay. Down an alley, I spot Commissary—it's happy hour, my favorite bartender is pouring large glasses of wine. In the distance, far to the west, I can just make out the gray stone outline of Georgetown. Looking out on the only city I'll ever call home, I pull out my cell.

A dozen faces fill the rectangles on the screen. Each face earns a salary north of a million dollars. I don't turn on my camera. My rectangle remains black. I'm where I belong. Where I've always belonged.

"I want to introduce Phil," Levick says. "My resident arsonist."

"Hello," my black box says.

"Phil works behind the scenes. After this call, he's going to go do his job," Levick says. "And you'll never hear from him again."

NOTES

Chapter 1: Of Marble and Giants

10 **"23 Most Important Comb-overs of Congress"**: Benny Johnson, "The 23 Most Important Comb-overs of Congress," *BuzzFeed News*, May 29, 2013, www.buzzfeednews.com/article /bennyjohnson/23-most-important-comb-overs-of-congress.

11 **"No, sir"**: "The Role of the Board of Directors in Enron's Collapse," n.d., GovInfo, www.govinfo.gov/content/pkg/CHRG -107shrg80300/html/CHRG-107shrg80300.htm.

17 **A. O. Scott in the *New York Times***: A. O. Scott, "With Soldiers in a Palace and Death in the Streets," *New York Times*, March 4, 2005, sec. Arts, www.nytimes.com/2005/03/04/movies /with-soldiers-in-a-palace-and-death-in-the-streets.html.

Chapter 2: Everyone Deserves Representation

22 **"Industry Money Fans Debate on Fish"**: Marian Burros, "Industry Money Fans Debate on Fish," *New York Times*, October 17, 2007, sec. Food, www.nytimes.com/2007/10/17/dining/17fish .html.

24 **"our people, planet, clients and communities"**: "About WPP: The Creative Transformation Company," WPP, n.d., www .wpp.com/en/about.

25   ***Thank You for Smoking***: Christopher Buckley, *Thank You for Smoking* (New York: Random House, 1994).

27   **"international voices remain silent"**: Matthew Slutsky and Peter Slutsky, "Barber Insults Islam, Receives Saudi Death Sentence," *HuffPost*, May 27, 2008, www.huffpost.com/entry /barber-insults-islam-rece_b_103742.

29   **"lies as truths—and with a smile"**: U.S. Department of State, "Faces of Kremlin Propaganda: Margarita Simonyan," Remarks and Releases, U.S. Department of State, August 31, 2022, www.state.gov/disarming-disinformation/faces-of-kremlin -propaganda-margarita-simonyan/.

31   **"effects by insensible or invisible means"**: "Influence," Online Etymology Dictionary, n.d. www.etymonline.com/word /influence.

38   **"Gaddafi: Provoking Russia"**: Muammar Gaddafi, "Gaddafi: Provoking Russia," *Washington Times*, December 23, 2008, www.washingtontimes.com/news/2008/dec/23/provoking -russia/.

44   **"Where, I ask, is the justice?"**: "Full Letter: FBI Sends Scathing Note to Scots over Pan Am 103 Bomber's Release," ABC News, August 22, 2009, abcnews.go.com/Politics/story?id =8390106.

46   **"Knock Off the Libya-bashing, Ortiz Says"**: Laura Rozen, "Knock Off the Libya-bashing, Ortiz Says," *Politico*, September 10, 2009, www.politico.com/blogs/laurarozen/0909/Rep_Ortiz_calls _for_end_to_the_Libya_bashing.html.

Chapter 3: The Doctor and Las Vegas

62   **"and the other way around"**: Staff Writer, "Revolving Door Links Airlines with FAA," *Columbus Dispatch*, April 20, 2008, www.dispatch.com/story/business/2008/04/20/revolving-door -links-airlines-with/24031290007/.

Chapter 4: No Fingerprints

70   **the rental broker told ABC**: Ari M. Brostoff, "Mystery Continues over Where Gadhafi Will Sleep," *Tablet*, September

23, 2009, www.tabletmag.com/sections/news/articles/mystery
-continues-over-where-gadhafi-will-sleep.

70 **wall hangings decorated with tiny camels:** Helen Pidd,
"Muammar Gaddafi's Tent Finds Home on Donald Trump's
Estate," *Guardian*, September 23, 2009, sec. World news, www
.theguardian.com/world/2009/sep/23/muammar-gaddafi-tent
-trump-estate.

70 **"everything in your power" to send Gaddafi packing:**
Paul Harris, "Muammar Gaddafi's Campsite Raises Hackles in
Smalltown America," *Guardian*, September 23, 2009, sec. US
News, www.theguardian.com/world/2009/sep/23/bedford-upset
-with-gaddafi-tent.

73 **"As an interview, he is the worst":** "CNN Official Interview:
Larry King 'Gadhafi Worst Interview Ever,'" YouTube, www
.youtube.com/watch?v=I0ycZlXDfQg.

76 **"but I can't think of many":** Matt Labash, "To the Shores
of Tripoli," *Weekly Standard*, December 14, 2009, www
.washingtonexaminer.com/weekly-standard/to-the-shores-of
-tripoli-272311.

Chapter 5: Thanks, Michelle

90 **Detroit urban legend:** Elisha Anderson, "Unsolved Slaying
of Stripper Tamara Greene Gets National Audience in Podcast,"
Detroit Free Press, February 7, 2019, www.freep.com/story/news
/local/michigan/detroit/2019/02/07/tamara-greene-crimetown
-podcast-detroit/2789295002/.

92 **"promoting a fair, modern marketplace that works for
all Americans":** "About Us," Free and Fair Markets Initiative,
freeandfairmarketsinitiative.org/about-us/.

93 **"Take Down Amazon Is Funded by Amazon's Biggest
Rivals":** James V. Grimaldi, "A 'Grass Roots' Campaign to Take
Down Amazon Is Funded by Amazon's Biggest Rivals," *Wall
Street Journal*, September 20, 2019, sec. Business, www.wsj.com
/articles/a-grassroots-campaign-to-take-down-amazon-is-funded
-by-amazons-biggest-rivals-11568989838.

96 **"A Rose in the Desert":** Joan Juliet Buck, "Asma Al-Assad:

A Rose in the Desert," *Vogue*, March 2011, reprinted online at www
.gawker.com/asma-al-assad-a-rose-in-the-desert-1265002284.

98   **internal document leaked by Julian Assange and
WikiLeaks:** Michael Moynihan, "Opinion—Washington's Syria
Lobbyists: 'Hard Power Necessary to Quell Rebellion,'" *Washington Post*, June 29, 2023, www.washingtonpost.com/blogs/right
-turn/post/washingtons-syria-lobbyists-hard-power-necessary
-to-quell-rebellion/2012/07/06/gJQA0jBWSW_blog.html.

103 **"and the state of Qatar," it begins:** Louise Radnofsky,
"Advocate for Libya, Syria Failed to File Disclosures," *Wall Street
Journal*, September 9, 2011, sec. Business, www.wsj.com/articles
/SB10001424053111904103404576557001732536530.

105 **played on Libyan state-run TV:** Joseph Logan, "Libyan TV
Carries Audio of Gaddafi Taunting NATO," Reuters, May 13, 2011,
sec. World News, www.reuters.com/article/us-libya/libyan-tv
-carries-audio-of-gaddafi-taunting-nato-idUSTRE7270JP20110513.

105 **"Do you know right from wrong?":** David Williams, "Who
Shot Gaddafi? New Video Shows Blood Pouring from Dictator Immediately Before Death but Mystery Surrounds Coup de
Grace," *Daily Mail*, October 20, 2011, www.dailymail.co.uk/news
/article-2051361/GADDAFI-DEAD-VIDEO-Dictator-begs-life
-summary-execution.html.

Chapter 6: The Government v. the Internet

110 **travels with a life-size statue of the alien from *Predator*:** Daniel Miller and Matthew Belloni, "Megaupload's Kim
Dotcom: Inside the Wild Life and Dramatic Fall of the Nerd
Who Burned Hollywood," *The Hollywood Reporter*, May 2, 2012,
www.hollywoodreporter.com/news/general-news/kim-dotcom
-megaupload-piracy-steve-jobs-kanye-west-kim-kardashian
-318376/.

110 **sent twenty million dollars to Greenpeace:** Sean Gallagher, "The Fast, Fabulous, Allegedly Fraudulent Life of Megaupload's Kim Dotcom," *Wired*, January 26, 2012, www.wired.com
/2012/01/kim-dotcom/.

110 **accessing classified military intel on Saddam Hussein:**
Alexander Gutzmer, "Schwere Vorwürfe gegen Letsbuyit-
Retter," *Die Welt*, November 16, 2001, www.welt.de/print-wams
/article608961/Schwere-Vorwuerfe-gegen-Letsbuyit-Retter.html.

110 **sabotaged the credit rating of former German chancellor Helmut Kohl:** John Cassy, Julia Snoddy, and Simon Bow-
ers, "White Knight for Letsbuyit," *Guardian*, January 25, 2001,
sec. Technology, www.theguardian.com/technology/2001/jan/25
/newmedia.business.

110 **"Royal Highness Kimble the First":** Rebecca Lewis, "Multi-
Millionaire Hacker Buys Chrisco Mansion," *NZ Herald*, September 12, 2023, www.nzherald.co.nz/nz/multi-millionaire-hacker
-buys-chrisco-mansion/DUMIN52RIKFIVWC57ZQCCKA4BM/.

110 **"(spelling out 'Linux' with bullet holes)":** Gallagher,
"The Fast, Fabulous, Allegedly Fraudulent Life of Megaupload's
Kim Dotcom."

111 **"Respect me because I can teach you":** David Simpson,
"6 Outrageous Kim Dotcom Moments," *Hollywood Reporter*,
May 2, 2012, www.hollywoodreporter.com/gallery/kim-dotcom
-outrageous-moments-318685/3-no-1-ranked-player-in-the-world
-at-modern-warfare-3/.

111 **"a PR man's nightmare and a journalist's dream":**
Amanda Hall, "City Profile: From Convicted Hacker to Dotcom
Backer," *Telegraph* (UK), January 28, 2001.

111 **cost the U.S. film industry around $29.2 billion per
year:** Ana Dascalescu, "MPA Says Online Piracy Is Responsible for 230,000 and 560,000 Jobs Lost in the US," TechTheLead,
October 11, 2022, https://techthelead.com/mpa-says-online
-piracy-is-responsible-for-230000-and-560000-jobs-lost-in-the
-us/#:~:text=%E2%80%9CIn%202020%2C%20there%20were%
20an.

113 **"Never let the truth get in the way of a good story":**
Stephanie Twining, "Belly Up: Jim Hewes of the Round Robin,"
Washingtonian, October 23, 2007, www.washingtonian.com
/2007/10/23/belly-up-jim-hewes-of-the-round-robin/.

115 **"Four percent of the internet. . . . It's a hit, it's a hit!":** "Kim Dotcom-Megaupload Song HD," YouTube, www.youtube.com/watch?v=o0Wvn-9BXVc.

116 **first case of confession via license plate:** Danny Vazquez, "Megaupload Founder Kim Dotcom Admits Guilt via License Plate," *Complex*, January 19, 2012, www.complex.com/sports/a/danny-vazquez/megaupload-founder-kim-dotcom-admits-guilt-via-license-plate.

124 **the price tag was $800,000:** David Armstrong, "Inside Purdue Pharma's Media Playbook: How It Planted the Opioid 'Anti-Story,'" ProPublica, November 19, 2019, www.propublica.org/article/inside-purdue-pharma-media-playbook-how-it-planted-the-opioid-anti-story.

124 **"oxycodone (OxyContin), morphine or methadone may be required":** Sally Satel, "Doctors Behind Bars," American Enterprise Institute, October 19, 2004, www.aei.org/articles/doctors-behind-bars/.

124 **died from opioid overdoses from 1999 to 2021:** Centers for Disease Control and Prevention, "Opioid Data Analysis and Resources: CDC's Response to the Opioid Overdose Epidemic—CDC," CDC, June 22, 2021, www.cdc.gov/opioids/data/analysis-resources.html.

126 **"Sacklers have been among our most generous supporters":** "The Metropolitan Museum of Art and Sackler Families Announce Removal of the Family Name in Dedicated Galleries," Press Release, Metropolitan Museum of Art, December 9, 2021, www.metmuseum.org/press/news/2021/the-met-and-sackler-families-announce-removal-of-the-family-name-in-dedicated-galleries.

127 **a DC firm with close ties to the Biden White House:** Daniel Lippman, "TikTok Hires Biden-Connected Firm as It Finds Itself Under D.C.'s Microscope," *Politico*, n.d., www.politico.com/news/2023/03/09/tiktok-biden-firm-dc-skdk-00086408.

Chapter 7: The Internet v. the Government

138 **"David vs. Goliath trade battle with the United States":** David McFadden, "APNewsBreak: Antigua to Seek

Sanctions Against US," AP, December 10, 2012, available at https: //www.smh.com.au/technology/apnewsbreak-antigua-to-seek -sanctions-against-us-20121210-2b44t.html.

140 **"Brandon Just Wants to Drive His Racecar":** Ben Smith, "Brandon Just Wants to Drive His Racecar," *New York Times*, December 19, 2021, sec. Business, www.nytimes.com/2021/12/19 /business/brandon-brown-lets-go-brandon.html.

140 **"A Fed Up Antigua Opens Its Doors to Megavideo":** Harold Lovell, "A Fed Up Antigua Opens Its Doors to Megavideo: Column," *USA Today*, February 1, 2013, www.usatoday.com/story /opinion/2013/02/01/antigua-world-trade-organization/1881557/.

147 **"A New Front in Global Trade Wars":** "Opinion: A New Front in Global Trade Wars," *New York Times*, February 8, 2013, sec. Opinion, www.nytimes.com/2013/02/08/opinion/a-new-front -in-global-trade-wars.html.

Chapter 8: Goodluck, Phil

163 **"All Malala Wants for Her Birthday Is Safe Return for Boko Haram Girls":** Charlotte Alter, "All Malala Wants for Her Birthday Is Safe Return for Boko Haram Girls," *Time*, July 14, 2014, time.com/2981368/malala-yousafzai-boko-haram -bringbackourgirls/.

164 **"their daughters will return home?":** "Malala Asks Jonathan to Meet Girls' Parents," News24, July 14, 2014, www.news24 .com/news24/malala-asks-jonathan-to-meet-girls-parents-20140714.

165 **"psychological terrorism":** "Nigeria's Goodluck Jonathan: #BringBackOurGirls 'Political,'" BBC News, July 15, 2014, sec. Africa, www.bbc.com/news/world-africa-28318259.

165 **writes the *Los Angeles Times*'s Robyn Dixon:** Robyn Dixon, "In Nigeria, Backlash Against U.S. Firm Hired to Improve Image," *Los Angeles Times*, July 17, 2014, www.latimes.com /world/africa/la-fg-nigeria-public-relations-20140717-story.html.

Chapter 9: Influence Games

185 **"Go past the Picasso, left at the Matisse":** Andrew Rawnsley, "Shepherd's Pie and Shampagne, Anyone?" *Guardian*, July 21,

2001, sec. UK News, www.theguardian.com/uk/2001/jul/22/archer
.conservatives.

190 **"She Hasn't Lost Yet"**: William Finnegan, "Taking Down Terrorists in Court," *New Yorker*, May 8, 2017, www.newyorker .com/magazine/2017/05/15/taking-down-terrorists-in-court.

Chapter 10: Target or Source

197 **"the Obama administration's most reactionary critics"**: Alex Thompson and Nick Niedzwiadek, "The Jennifer Rubin–WH Symbiosis." *West Wing Playbook, Politico,* September 16, 2021, www.politico.com/newsletters/west-wing-playbook/2021/09/16 /the-jennifer-rubin-wh-symbiosis-494364.

201 **exposing Mueller's probe into foreign influence in Washington:** Byron Tau, Rebecca Ballhaus, and Aruna Viswanatha, "Mueller Probe into U.A.E. Influence Broadens," *Wall Street Journal,* April 3, 2018, sec. Politics, www.wsj.com/articles /mueller-probe-into-u-a-e-influence-broadens-1522718922.

201 **"Mueller Asked About Money Flows to Israeli Social-Media Firm, Source Says"**: Michael Riley and Lauren Etter, "Mueller Asked About Money Flows to Israeli Social-Media Firm, Source Says," Bloomberg, May 22, 2018, www.bloomberg.com /politics/articles/2018–05–22/mueller-targeted-flows-of-money-to -israeli-social-media-company.

202 **Psy-Group's partnership with Cambridge Analytica:** Byron Tau and Rebecca Ballhaus, "Israeli Intelligence Company Formed Venture with Trump Campaign Firm Cambridge Analytica," *Wall Street Journal,* May 22, 2018, sec. Politics, www.wsj.com /articles/israeli-intelligence-company-formed-venture-with-trump -campaign-firm-cambridge-analytica-1527030765.

204 **"Qatar Sabotaged 2022 World Cup Rivals with 'Black Ops'"**: "Exclusive: Qatar Sabotaged 2022 World Cup Rivals with 'Black Ops,'" *Times* (UK), September 11, 2023, sec. News, www .thetimes.co.uk/article/exclusive-qatar-sabotaged-2022-world -cup-rivals-with-black-ops-glwl3kxkk#:~:text=Exclusive%3A%20 Qatar%20sabotaged%202022%20World%20Cup%20rivals%20 with%20.

206 **"Rick Gates Sought Online Manipulation Plans from Israeli Intelligence Firm for Trump Campaign":** Mark Mazzetti et al., "Rick Gates Sought Online Manipulation Plans from Israeli Intelligence Firm for Trump Campaign," *New York Times*, October 8, 2018, sec. U.S., www.nytimes.com/2018/10/08/us/politics/rick-gates-psy-group-trump.html#:~:text=WASHINGTON%20%E2%80%94%20A%20top%20Trump%20campaign.

Chapter 11: Deadline

215 **a damning portrait of Trump's overtures to the Libyan regime:** Daniel Wagner and Aram Roston, "The Donald and the Dictator," *BuzzFeed News*, June 7, 2016, www.buzzfeednews.com/article/danielwagner/how-trump-tried-to-get-qaddafis-cash.

216 **the two did business together:** Staff, "Full Transcript: First 2016 Presidential Debate," *Politico*, September 27, 2016, www.politico.com/story/2016/09/full-transcript-first-2016-presidential-debate-228761.

Chapter 12: Fix You

233 **Forty-eight thousand people in 2021:** Centers for Disease Control and Prevention, "Facts About Suicide," CDC, May 8, 2023, www.cdc.gov/suicide/facts/index.html.

233 **decreased suicidal ideation by at least 85 percent:** Meryl Kornfield, "Nothing Seemed to Treat Their Depression. Then They Tried Ketamine," *Washington Post*, September 12, 2022, www.washingtonpost.com/wellness/2022/09/12/ketamine-depression-treatment-research/.

233 **"Nothing Seemed to Treat Their Depression. Then They Tried Ketamine":** Kornfield, "Nothing Seemed to Treat Their Depression. Then They Tried Ketamine."

ACKNOWLEDGMENTS

First, I would like to thank my wife, Lindsay. I would not be here without her. If Howard Yoon hadn't talked her into this, it would not have happened. Howard also deserves a lot of the credit for this. I am not sure what regular agents do, but I have a feeling it is not this much. Then there are the two brothers who introduced me to the agent. I blame the two of you a great deal for this. Richard Levick was my mentor and I'm glad we made it to his part in the story, before doing our last story together, his obituary.

We tried to keep this book a secret for a long time. As a result, I had a lot of people read it and help with it. I want to thank you all for your patience with me. In no particular order: Kate, Liz, Maria, Chester, Raphael, Max, Michael, Adam, Kate, Michael, James, Louise, Megan, Byron, Denise, J.P., Ben, Ryan, Dan, Peter, Joy, Ashtan, Nancy, Jon, Lisa, Kaija, Stephen, Zach, Alice, Fred, Paul, Dave, Mark, Donna, Christa, Sean, and Matt.

Thanks to Vader for being willing to work ideas through with me at 3:00 a.m. when no one else would.

A special thank-you to my longtime lawyer David Saltzman. You know I'm always good for repeat business. Also, to Tim Duggan for taking a massive risk on a first-time author. Additionally, everyone at Henry Holt for their time, support, and commitment to this project. Also, if you need a fact checked, Hilary McClellen is who you should call.

Finally, I want to thank Kai Flanders. It was so much fun showing you this world of mayhem. Thank you for helping me communicate.

ABOUT THE AUTHOR

Phil Elwood is a public relations operative. He was born in New York City, grew up in Idaho, and moved to Washington, DC, at age twenty to intern for Senator Daniel Patrick Moynihan. He completed his undergraduate degree from Georgetown University and his graduate studies at the London School of Economics before starting his career at a small PR firm. Over the past two decades, Elwood has worked for some of the top—and bottom—PR firms in Washington. He lives in DC.